Selenium WebDriver Recipes in C#

Second Edition

Zhimin Zhan

Apress®

Selenium WebDriver Recipes in C#, Second Edition

Copyright © 2015 by Zhimin Zhan

ISBN-13 (pbk): 978-1-4842-1741-2

ISBN-13 (electronic): 978-1-4842-1742-9

Managing Director: Welmoed Spahr
Lead Editor: Steve Anglin
Technical Reviewers: Dolkun Tursun Tarim and Jerrel Blankenship
Editorial Board: Steve Anglin, Pramila Balan, Louise Corrigan, Jonathan Gennick,
    Robert Hutchinson, Celestin Suresh John, Michelle Lowman, James Markham,
    Susan McDermott, Matthew Moodie, Jeffrey Pepper, Douglas Pundick,
    Ben Renow-Clarke, Gwenan Spearing
Coordinating Editor: Mark Powers
Copy Editor: Teresa Horton
Compositor: SPi Global
Indexer: SPi Global
Artist: SPi Global

Distributed to the book trade worldwide by Springer Nature, 233 Spring Street, 6th Floor, New York, NY 10013. Phone 1-800-SPRINGER, fax (201) 348-4505, e-mail orders-ny@springer-sbm.com, or visit www.springeronline.com. Apress Media, LLC is a California LLC and the sole member (owner) is Springer Science + Business Media Finance Inc (SSBM Finance Inc). SSBM Finance Inc is a Delaware corporation.

For information on translations, please e-mail rights@apress.com, or visit www.apress.com.

Apress and friends of ED books may be purchased in bulk for academic, corporate, or promotional use. eBook versions and licenses are also available for most titles. For more information, reference our Special Bulk Sales–eBook Licensing web page at www.apress.com/bulk-sales.

Any source code or other supplementary materials referenced by the author in this text is available to readers at www.apress.com/9781484217412. For detailed information about how to locate your book's source code, go to www.apress.com/source-code/. Readers can also access source code at SpringerLink in the Supplementary Material section for each chapter.

I dedicate this book to my parents, who had the unusual belief that I could achieve something with computers since I was in high shcool. They bought me my first computer (Apple IIe) in 1988, which was a big deal back then, costing half a family's yearly income.

Contents at a Glance

Contents

About the Author

Zhimin Zhan is the founder and Continuous Integration Officer of AgileWay Pty Ltd, Australia. As an advisor and coach, he helps organzations by implementing test automation with Continuous Integration using open technologies such as Selenium WebDriver and Watir. Zhimin is the creator of TestWise, the next-generation functional testing tool that supports functional test refactorings, and is a frequent speaker and writer. He shares his test automation and CI experience at `testwisely.com`.

About the Technical Reviewer

Dolkun Tursun Tarim is a senior quality assurance test automation engineer, and the founder of Selenium Master. Mr. Tarim has more than 10 years of progressive experiences in managing quality assurance test automation teams and projects, and developing QTP, LoadRunner, JMeter, and Selenium automation frameworks with VBScript, .Net, Java, Python, and Python Robot Framework languages. He has worked on various automated functional and performance testing projects utilizing commercial and open source test automation applications and framework APIs. In his free time, he posts instructional articles about selenium API on his company website, `http://www.seleniummaster.com` and assist team members on projects.

Acknowledgments

I wish to personally thank the following people for their contributions to my inspiration and knowledge and other help in creating this book:

Thanks to all the readers of the first edition; their feedback, suggestions and encourgement inspired me to make this new version of the book more comphrensive.

Thank you to my editor, Mark Powers, for such efficient collaboration during the book writing process, which frankly I still don't know much. Mark and his support team carefully managed the manuscript development process and publication side of things.

Thank you for the technical reviewers: Lien Nguyen, Dolkun Tarim, and Jerrel Blankenship, who made great suggestions and spotted many errors and omissions.

Finally, a very big thank you to my family. Without their support and patience, I couldn't have finished this book.

Preface

After observing many failed test automation attempts by using expensive commercial test automation tools, I am delighted to see that the value of open-source testing frameworks has finally been recognized. I still remember the day (a rainy day at a Gold Coast hotel in 2011) when I found out that the Selenium WebDriver was the most wanted testing skill in terms of the number of job ads on Australia's top job-seeking site.

Now Selenium WebDriver is big in the testing world. Software giants such as Facebook and LinkedIn use it, as immensely-comprehensive automated UI testing enables them to push out releases several times a day. However, from my observation, many software projects, while using Selenium WebDriver, are not getting much value from test automation, and certainly nowhere near its potential. A clear sign of this is that the regression testing is not conducted on a daily basis (if test automation is done well, it will happen naturally).

Among the factors contributing to test automation failures, a key one is that automation testers lack sufficient knowledge in the test framework. It is quite common to see some testers or developers get excited when they first create a few simple test cases and see them run in a browser. However, it does not take long for them to encounter some obstacles, such as being unable to automate certain operations. If one step cannot be automated, the whole test case does not work, which is the nature of test automation. Searching solutions online is not always successful, and posting questions on forums and waiting can be frustrating (usually, very few people seek professional help from test automation coaches). Not surprisingly, many projects eventually gave up test automation or just used it for testing a handful of scenarios.

The motivation of this book is to help motivated testers work better with Selenium. The book contains over 170 recipes for web application tests with Selenium. If you have read one of my other books, *Practical Web Test Automation*, you probably know my style: practical. I will let the test scripts do most of the talking. These recipe test scripts are "live," as I have created the target test site and included offline test web pages. With both, you can:

1. Identify your issue

2. Find the recipe

3. Run the test case

4. See test execution in your browser

Who Should Read This Book

This book is for testers or programmers who are writing (or want to learn) automated tests with Selenium WebDriver. In order to get the most of this book, basic C# coding skill is required.

How to Read This Book

Usually, a "recipe" book is a reference book. Readers can go directly to the part that interests them. For example, if you are testing a multiple select list and don't know how, you can look it up in the Table of Contents, and then go to the chapter. This book supports this style of reading. Since the recipes are arranged according to their levels of complexity, readers will also be able to work through the book from the front to back if they are looking to learn test automation with Selenium WebDriver.

Recipe Test Scripts

To help readers to learn more effectively, this book has a dedicated site that contains the recipe test scripts and related resources.

As an old saying goes, "There's more than one way to skin a cat." You can achieve the same testing outcome with test scripts implemented in different ways. The recipe test scripts in this book are written for simplicity, there is always room for improvement. But for many, to understand the solution quickly and get the job done are probably more important.

If you have a better and simpler way, please let me know.

All recipe test scripts are Selenium WebDriver 2 compliant, and can be run on Firefox, Chrome and Internet Explorer on multiple platforms.

Send Me Feedback

I would appreciate your comments, suggestions, reports on errors in the book and the recipe test scripts. You may submit errata at the book's Apress product page, located at www.apress.com/9781484217412.

Zhimin Zhan
Brisbane, Australia

■ ■ ■

CHAPTER 1

Introduction

Selenium WebDriver is a free and open source library for automated testing web applications. I assume that you have had some knowledge of Selenium WebDriver, based on the fact that you picked up this book (or opened it in your eBook reader).

Selenium was originally created in 2004 by Jason Huggins, who was later joined by his other ThoughtWorks colleagues. Selenium supports all major browsers and tests can be written in many programming languages and run on Windows, Linux, and Macintosh platforms.

Selenium 2 is merged with another test framework WebDriver (that's why you see 'selenium-webdriver') led by Simon Stewart at Google (he now works at Facebook), and Selenium 2.0 was released in July 2011. I use the names Selenium, WebDriver, and Selenium WebDriver interchangeably in this book.

Selenium Language Bindings

Selenium tests can be written in multiple programming languages such as Java, C#, Python, and Ruby (the core ones). All examples in this book are written in Selenium with C# binding. As you will see in the examples that follow, the use of Selenium in different bindings is very similar. Once you master one, you can apply it to others quite easily. Take a look at a simple Selenium test script in four different language bindings: C#, Java, Python, and Ruby.

C#

```
using System;

using OpenQA.Selenium;
using OpenQA.Selenium.Firefox;
using OpenQA.Selenium.Support.UI;

class GoogleSearch
{
  static void Main()
  {
    // Create a new instance of the driver
    // Notice that the remainder of the code relies on the interface,
    // not the implementation.
    IWebDriver driver = new FirefoxDriver();
```

```
    // And now use this to visit Google
    driver.Navigate().GoToUrl("http://www.google.com");

    // Find the text input element by its name
    IWebElement query = driver.FindElement(By.Name("q"));

    // Enter something to search for
    query.SendKeys("Hello Selenium WebDriver!");

    // Submit the form based on an element in the form
    query.Submit();

    // Check the title of the page
    Console.WriteLine(driver.Title);
  }
}
```

Java

```
import org.openqa.selenium.By;
import org.openqa.selenium.WebDriver;
import org.openqa.selenium.WebElement;
import org.openqa.selenium.firefox.FirefoxDriver;

public class GoogleSearch  {
  public static void main(String[] args) {
    WebDriver driver = new FirefoxDriver();
    driver.get("http://www.google.com");
    WebElement element = driver.findElement(By.name("q"));
    element.sendKeys("Hello Selenium WebDriver!");
    element.submit();
    System.out.println("Page title is: " + driver.getTitle());
  }
}
```

Python

```
from selenium import webdriver

driver = webdriver.Firefox()
driver.get("http://www.google.com")

elem = driver.find_element_by_name("q")
elem.send_keys("Hello WebDriver!")
elem.submit()

print(driver.title)
```

Ruby

```
require "selenium-webdriver"

driver = Selenium::WebDriver.for :firefox
driver.navigate.to "http://www.google.com"

element = driver.find_element(:name, 'q')
element.send_keys "Hello Selenium WebDriver!"
element.submit

puts driver.title
```

Set up the Development Environment

Most C# programmers develop C# code in Microsoft Visual Studio. I use Visual Studio Community 2015 as the integrated development environment (IDE) of choice for this book, as it is free.

Prerequisites

- Download and install Visual Studio Community 2015.

- Make sure your target browser is installed, such as Chrome or Firefox.

Set up Visual Studio Solution

1. Create a new project in Visual Studio.

    Select Templates ➤ Visual C# ➤ Test ➤ Unit Test Project, as shown in Figure 1-1.

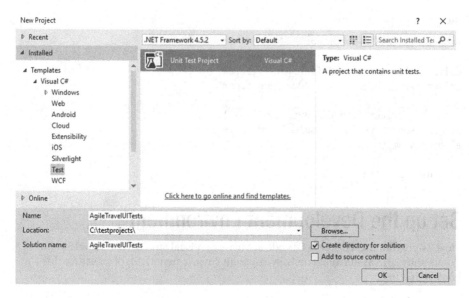

Figure 1-1. *Selecting a template for a new Visual Studio project*

You will see the project skeleton created, as shown in Figure 1-2.

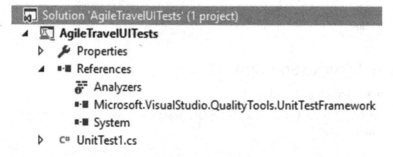

Figure 1-2. *Skeleton for a new project*

2. Add the Selenium WebDriver package to the project.

Run the following command in the Package Manager Console (select Tools ➤ NuGet Package Manager ➤ Package Manager Console; see Figure 1-3):

```
PM> Install-Package Selenium.WebDriver
```

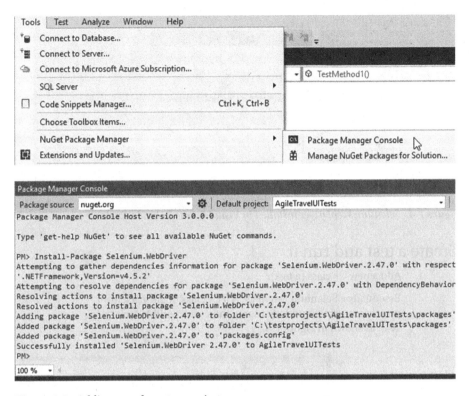

Figure 1-3. Adding a package to a project

Also install Selenium.Support, which includes helper .NET classes for the Selenium WebDriver application programming interface (API), using this command:

```
PM> Install-Package Selenium.Support
```

Figure 1-4 shows what looks like in Visual Studio Solution Explorer after Selenium WebDriver is installed.

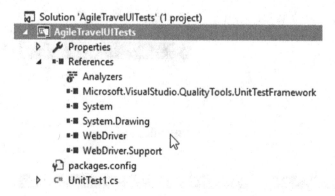

Figure 1-4. *Selenium WebDriver installed in Visual Studio Solution Explorer*

Create a test and run it

1. Add a new C# class (a test).

   Essentially a Selenium test in C# is a C# class. Right-click the project name in Solution Explorer, then select Add ➤ Unit Test, as shown in Figure 1-5.

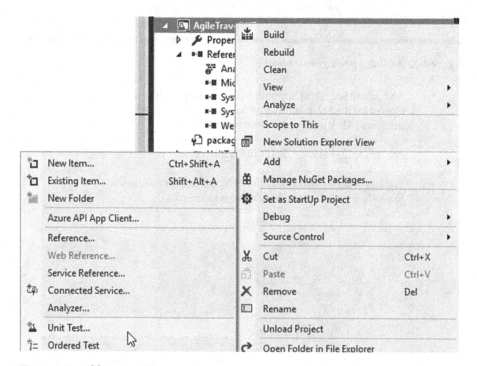

Figure 1-5. *Adding a unit test*

A new unit test file is created (named UnitTest1.cs or UnitTest2.cs if UnitTest1.cs already exists). Rename it (press F2 and enter a name in camel case, such as GoogleSearchTest), as shown in Figure 1-6.

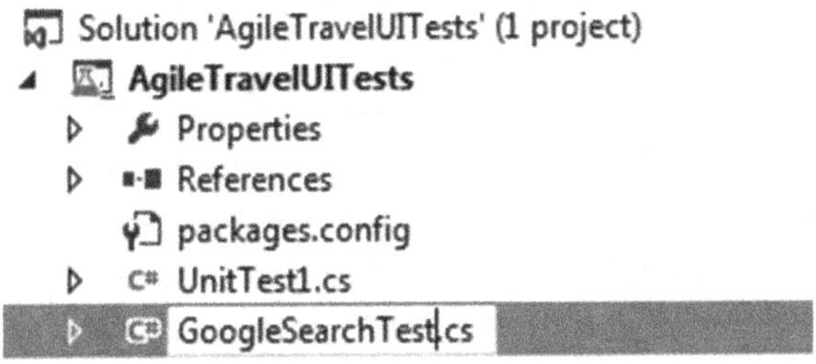

- 🗔 Solution 'AgileTravelUITests' (1 project)
- ◢ 🗔 AgileTravelUITests
  - ▷ 🔧 Properties
  - ▷ ■-■ References
  - 🗐 packages.config
  - ▷ C# UnitTest1.cs
  - ▷ C# GoogleSearchTest.cs

Figure 1-6. *Renaming the new unit test file*

2. Create a test case.

   For simplicity, paste a Google Search test case script into the editor, similar to the one shown in Figure 1-7.

```
[TestClass]
public class GoogleSearchTest
{
    [TestMethod]
    public void TestSearch()
    {
        IWebDriver driver = new FirefoxDriver();

        // And now use this to visit Google
        driver.Navigate().GoToUrl("http://www.google.com");

        // Find the text input element by its name
        IWebElement element = driver.FindElement(By.Name("q"));

        // Enter something to search for
        element.SendKeys("Hello Selenium WebDriver!");

        // Now submit the form.
        element.Submit();

    }
}
```

Figure 1-7. *Creating a test case*

The several red underlines, like the one shown in Figure 1-8, indicate compiling errors. In this case, the Selenium classes were not loaded. To fix this, right-click these red underlines and select Resolve.

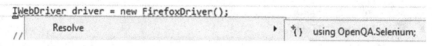

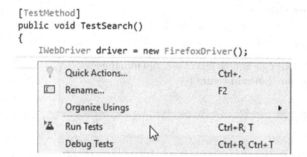

Figure 1-8. *Resolving a compiling error*

3. Run the test.

    Right-click the editor and select Run Tests, as shown in Figure 1-9.

```
[TestMethod]
public void TestSearch()
{
    IWebDriver driver = new FirefoxDriver();
```

💡 Quick Actions...	Ctrl+.	
▭ Rename...	F2	
Organize Usings	▶	
ᴤ Run Tests	Ctrl+R, T	
Debug Tests	Ctrl+R, Ctrl+T	

Figure 1-9. *Running the test*

A Firefox browser will open. Do a Google search in the browser, as we indicated in our instructions (in `GoogleSearchTest.cs`).

Click the Test Explorer tab to see the test execution result, as shown in Figure 1-10.

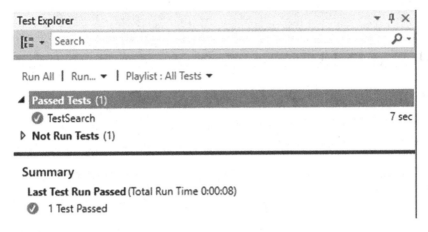

Figure 1-10. Checking the test execution result

Cross-Browser Testing

The biggest advantage of Selenium over other web test frameworks, in my opinion, is that it supports all major web browsers: Firefox, Chrome, and Internet Explorer. The browser market nowadays is more diversified (based on the StatsCounter, the usage shares in September 2015 for Chrome, Internet Explorer, and Firefox are 53.1%, 15.7%, and 15.8%, respectively). It is logical that all external-facing web sites require serious cross-browser testing. Selenium is a natural choice for this purpose, as it far exceeds other commercial tools and free test frameworks.

Firefox

Selenium supports Firefox out of the box, so as long as you have Firefox (a recent version) installed, you are ready to go. The following test script opens a web site in a new Firefox window.

```
using OpenQA.Selenium.Firefox;
// ...
IWebDriver driver = new FirefoxDriver();
```

Chrome

To run Selenium tests in Google Chrome, besides the Chrome browser itself, ChromeDriver needs to be installed.

Installing ChromeDriver is easy. go to http://chromedriver.storage.googleapis.com/index.html, as shown in Figure 1-11.

Index of /2.13/

Name	Last modified	Size	
Parent Directory		-	
chromedriver_linux32.zip	2014-12-10 13:17:59	2.23MB	187dbe7973c
chromedriver_linux64.zip	2014-12-10 13:22:58	2.11MB	fcfd9933307
chromedriver_mac32.zip	2014-12-10 14:02:54	3.27MB	e37a65a1be6
chromedriver_win32.zip	2014-12-10 13:40:47	2.30MB	ae85407694c
notes.txt	2014-12-10 13:18:01	0.01MB	a57d33a29c8

Figure 1-11. *Downloading ChromeDriver*

Download the appropriate file for your target platform, unzip it, and put the chromedriver executable in your PATH. To verify the installation, open a command window, and execute the command chromedriver. The result will look like Figure 1-12.

```
C:\>chromedriver
Starting ChromeDriver 2.13.307647 (5a7d0541ebc58e69994a6fb2ed930f45261f3c29) on port 9515
Only local connections are allowed.
```

Figure 1-12. *Verifying installation*

The following test script opens a site in a new Chrome browser window and closes it one second later.

```
using OpenQA.Selenium.Chrome;
//...
IWebDriver driver = new ChromeDriver();
```

Internet Explorer

Selenium requires IEDriverServer to drive the Internet Explorer browser. Its installation process is very similar to that for chromedriver. IEDriverServer is available at http://www.seleniumhq.org/download/. Choose the right file based on your version of Windows (32 or 64 bit), as shown in Figure 1-13.

Download version 2.44.0 for (recommended) 32 bit Windows IE or 64 bit Windows IE
CHANGELOG

Figure 1-13. *Downloading IEDriverServer*

When a test starts to execute in Internet Explorer, before navigating to the target test site, you will see the message shown in Figure 1-14.

Figure 1-14. Starting a test in Internet Explorer

Using Internet Explorer 9, if you get an Unexpected Error Launching Internet Explorer. Protected Mode Must Be Set to the Same Value (Enabled or Disabled) for All Zones" error message, go to Internet Options, select each zone (see Figure 1-15), and make sure they are all set to the same mode (Protected or not).

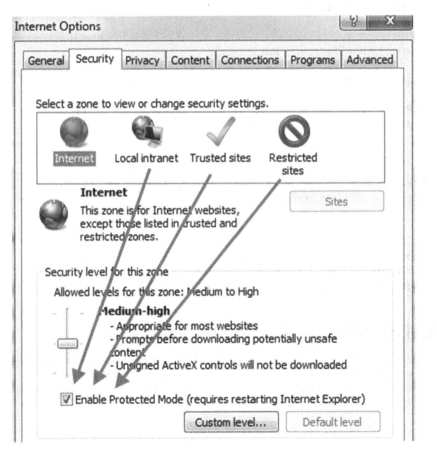

Figure 1-15. Setting each zone to the same mode

Further configuration is required for Internet Explorer 10 and Internet Explorer 11. See IE and IEDriverServer Runtime Configuration (https://code.google.com/p/selenium/wiki/InternetExplorerDriver#Required_Configuration) for details.

```
using OpenQA.Selenium.IE;
//...
IWebDriver driver = new InternetExplorerDriver();
```

Edge

Microsoft Edge is the new default web browser for Windows 10. To drive Edge with WebDriver, you need to download the MicrosoftWebDriver server. After installation, you will find the executable (MicrosoftWebDriver.exe) in the Program Files folder.

```
using System.IO;
using OpenQA.Selenium.Edge;
// ...

string serverPath = "Microsoft Web Driver";

if (System.Environment.Is64BitOperatingSystem)
{
  serverPath = Path.Combine(System.Environment.ExpandEnvironmentVariables
  ("%ProgramFiles(x86)%"), serverPath);
}
else
{
  serverPath = Path.Combine(System.Environment.ExpandEnvironmentVariables
  ("%ProgramFiles%"), serverPath);
}

// location for MicrosoftWebDriver.exe
EdgeOptions options = new EdgeOptions();
options.PageLoadStrategy = EdgePageLoadStrategy.Eager;
IWebDriver driver = new EdgeDriver(serverPath, options);
```

Visual Studio Unit Testing Framework

The preceding examples drive browsers. Strictly speaking, they are not tests. To make the effective use of Selenium scripts for testing, we need to put them in a test framework that defines test structures and provides assertions (performing checks in test scripts). Here is an example using Visual Studio Unit Testing Framework.

```
using System;
using Microsoft.VisualStudio.TestTools.UnitTesting;
using OpenQA.Selenium;
```

```
using OpenQA.Selenium.Firefox;
using OpenQA.Selenium.IE;
using OpenQA.Selenium.Chrome;
using System.Collections.ObjectModel;

[TestClass]
public class GoogleSearchDifferentBrowsersTest {

    [TestMethod]
    public void TestInIE() {
        IWebDriver driver = new InternetExplorerDriver();
        driver.Navigate().GoToUrl("http://testwisely.com/demo");
        System.Threading.Thread.Sleep(1000);
        driver.Quit();
    }

    [TestMethod]
    public void TestInFirefox() {
        IWebDriver driver = new FirefoxDriver();
        driver.Navigate().GoToUrl("http://testwisely.com/demo");
        System.Threading.Thread.Sleep(1000);
        driver.Quit();
    }

    [TestMethod]
    public void TestInChrome() {
        IWebDriver driver = new ChromeDriver();
        driver.Navigate().GoToUrl("http://testwisely.com/demo");
        System.Threading.Thread.Sleep(1000);
        driver.Quit();
    }

    [TestMethod]
    public void TestInChrome() {
        // Default option, MicrosoftWebDriver.exe must be in PATH
        IWebDriver driver = new EdgeDriver();
        driver.Navigate().GoToUrl("http://testwisely.com/demo");
        System.Threading.Thread.Sleep(1000);
        driver.Quit();
    }
}
```

@TestMethod annotates a test case, in a format of TestCapitalCase. You can find more about Visual Studio Unit Test Framework from its home page. However, I honestly don't think it is necessary. The part used for test scripts is quite intuitive. After studying and trying some examples, you will be quite comfortable with it.

Visual Studio Unit Testing Framework Fixtures

If you have worked with xUnit before, you must know the setUp() and tearDown() fixtures, which are called before or after every test. In Visual Studio Unit Test Framework, by using annotations ([ClassInitialize], [TestInitialize], [TestCleanup], [ClassCleanup]), you can choose the name for the fixtures. Here are mine:

```
[ClassInitialize]
public static void BeforeAll() {
   // run before all test cases
}

[TestInitialize]
public void Before() {
   // run before each test case
}

[TestMethod]
public void TestCase1() {
   // one test case
}

[TestMethod]
public void TestCase2() {
   // another test case
}

[TestCleanup]
public void After() {
   // run after each test case
}

[ClassCleanup]
public static void AfterAll() {
   // run after all test cases, typically, close browser
}
```

Note that ClassCleanup does not guarantee all tests from one test class have been executed before a new test class is initialized. What does this mean to your execution? If you run one test case or all test cases in one test class, [ClassCleanup] is invoked as you expected. However, when you run several test classes in one go, the time of invocation of [ClassCleanup] is nondeterministic (which leaves many browser windows open). Read this MSDN blog post for explanation: ClassCleanup May Run Later Than You Think (http://blogs.msdn.com/b/ploeh/archive/2007/01/06/ classcleanupmayrunlaterthanyouthink.aspx).

Alternative Framework NUnit

NUnit, inspired by JUnit, is an open source unit testing framework for Microsoft .NET. If you have used JUnit before, you will find similarities in NUnit. Personally, I like NUnit more than Visual Studio Unit Test Framework. In particular, it's more flexible to execute tests from the command line with Junit-style test reports (which can be easily integrated with CI Servers).

However, you will need to spend some effort getting NUnit to work with Visual Studio.

Run Recipe Scripts

Test scripts for all recipes can be downloaded from the book site. They are all in ready-to-run state. I include the target web pages as well as Selenium test scripts. There are two kinds of target web pages: local HTML files and web pages on a live site. Running the tests written for live sites requires an Internet connection.

Run Tests in Visual Studio

The most convenient way to run one test case or a test suite is to do it in an IDE. (When you have a large number of test cases, the most effective way to run all tests is a Continuous Integration process.)

Find the Test Case

You can locate the recipe either by following the chapter or searching by name. There are more than 150 test cases in the test project. Being able to quickly navigate to the test case is important when you have developed a large number of test cases.

Visual Studio includes the Navigate To command. Its default keyboard shortcut is Ctrl +, resulting the display shown in Figure 1-16.

Figure 1-16. *Using the Navigate To command*

The pop-up window shown in Figure 1-17 lists all artefacts (test cases, classes) in the project for your selection. The finding starts as soon as you type.

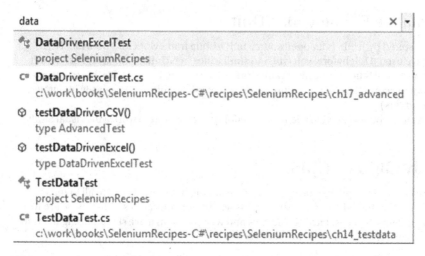

Figure 1-17. *Searching for a test case*

Run Individual Test Case

Move the pointer to a line within a test case, right–click, and select Run Tests, shown in Figure 1-18, to run this case.

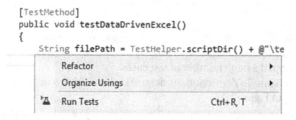

Figure 1-18. *Running the selected case*

Figure 1-19 is a screenshot of the execution panel when one test case failed.

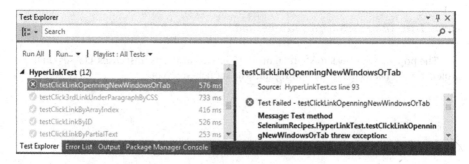

Figure 1-19. *Test Explorer showing a failed case*

Run all Test Cases in a Test Script File

You can also run all test cases in the currently opened test script file by right-clicking anywhere in the editor and selecting Run Tests (see Figure 1-20).

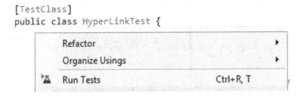

Figure 1-20. Running all test cases

Figure 1-21 is a screenshot of the execution panel when all test cases in a test script file passed.

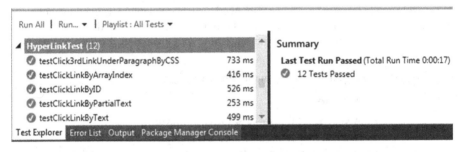

Figure 1-21. Test Explorer showing all cases have passed

Run all Tests

You can also run all the test cases in a Visual Studio project. First, set the main project by selecting Tools ➤ Run ➤ All Tests, as shown in Figure 1-22.

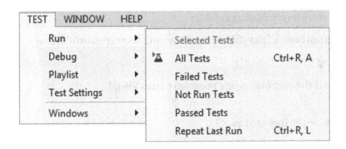

Figure 1-22. Running all test cases in a project

17

Figure 1-23 is a screenshot of the test results panel after running more than 100 tests across dozens of test files.

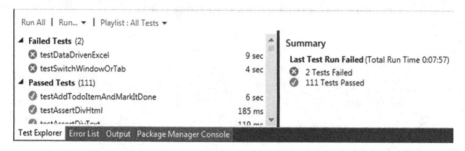

Figure 1-23. *Test Explorer results of running all tests in a project*

Run Tests from the Command Line

One key advantage of open source test frameworks, such as Selenium, is freedom. You can edit the test scripts in any text editors and run them from a command line.

To run a C# class, you need to be compile it first. (Within an IDE, the IDE will do it for you automatically.)

1. Open a Visual Studio command prompt.

    - **In Windows 7**

        Click Start ➤ All Programs ➤ Visual Studio 2015 ➤ Visual Studio Tools, and choose Developer Command Prompt for VS2015.

    - **In Windows 8 or Windows 10**

        Search for and run Developer Command Prompt for VS2015.

2. By default, the Visual Studio command prompt opens to the following folder:

    `C:\Program Files (x86)\Microsoft Visual Studio 14.0>`

3. Change the directory to your solution folder:

    `cd C:\books\SeleniumRecipes-C#\recipes\SeleniumRecipes\bin\Debug`

4. Run all tests using VSTest.Console.

    VSTest.Console is the command-line program to run Visual Studio tests.

    `vstest.console SeleniumRecipes.dll`

    Example output is shown in Figure 1-24.

```
Total tests: 113. Passed: 110. Failed: 3. Skipped: 0.
Test Run Failed.
Test execution time: 8.8321 Minutes
```

Figure 1-24. *Example output after running a test case*

5. Run individual test cases.

   The following command runs two test cases in different files.

   ```
   vstest.console SeleniumRecipes.dll /Tests:TestSendSpe
   cialKeys,TestModalDialog
   ```

   This is the sample output:

   ```
   Passed    TestModalDialog
   Passed    TestSendSpecialKeys

   Total tests: 2. Passed: 2. Failed: 0. Skipped: 0.
   Test Run Successful.
   Test execution time: 10.9916 Seconds
   ```

   For more VSTest.Console options, visit
   https://msdn.microsoft.com/en-us/library/jj155796.aspx.

■ ■ ■

CHAPTER 2

Locating Web Elements

As you might have already figured out, to drive an element in a page, we need to find it first. Selenium uses what are called locators to find and match the elements on a web page. There are eight locators in Selenium, as listed in Table 2-1.

Table 2-1. *Locators in Selenium*

Locator	Example
ID	FindElement(By.Id("user"))
Name	FindElement(By.Name("username"))
Link Text	FindElement(By.LinkText("Login"))
Partial Link Text	FindElement(By.PartialLinkText("Next"))
XPath	FindElement(By.Xpath("//div[@id="login"]/input"))
Tag Name	FindElement(By.TagName("body"))
Class Name	FindElement(By.ClassName("table"))
CSS	FindElement(By.CssSelector, "#login > input[type="text"]"))

You can use any one of them to narrow down to the element you are looking for.

Start browser

Testing web sites starts with a browser.

```
static WebDriver driver = new FirefoxDriver();
driver.Navigate().GoToUrl("http://testwisely.com/demo")
```

Use ChromeDriver and IEDriver for testing in Google Chrome and Internet Explorer, respectively.

```
driver = new InternetExplorerDriver();
driver = new ChromeDriver();
```

I recommend, for beginners, closing the browser window at the end of a test case, so that you don't end up with many browser windows after executing a number of tests.

```
driver.Quit();
```

There is also `driver.Close()`, which closes the browser window with the focus. `driver.Quit()` closes all browser windows and ends the WebDriver session.

Find element by ID

Using IDs is the easiest and the safest way to locate an element in a page. If a web page is W3C HTML conformed, the IDs should be unique and identified in web controls. In comparison to texts, test scripts that use IDs are less prone to application changes (e.g., developers might decide to change the label, but are less likely to change the ID).

```
driver.FindElement(By.Id("submit_btn")).Click();    // Button
driver.FindElement(By.Id("cancel_link")).Click();   // Link
driver.FindElement(By.Id("username")).SendKeys("agileway");  // Textfield
driver.FindElement(By.Id("alert_div")).getText();   // HTML Div element
```

Find element by Name

The name attributes are used in form controls such as text fields and radio buttons. The values of the name attributes are passed to the server when a form is submitted. In terms of least likelihood of a change, the name attribute is probably only second to ID.

```
driver.FindElement(By.Name("comment")).SendKeys("Selenium Cool");
```

Find element by Link Text

For hyperlinks only, using a link's text is probably the most direct way to click a link, as it is what we see on the page.

```
driver.FindElement(By.LinkText("Cancel")).Click();
```

Find element by Partial Link Text

Selenium allows you to identify a hyperlink control with partial text. This can be quite useful when the text is dynamically generated. In other words, the text on one web page might be different on your next visit. We might be able to use the common text shared by these dynamically generated link texts to identify them.

```
// will click the "Cancel" link
driver.FindElement(By.PartialLinkText("ance")).Click();
```

Find element by XPath

XPath, the XML Path Language, is a query language for selecting nodes from an XML document. When a browser renders a web page, it parses it into a DOM tree or similar. XPath can be used to refer to a certain node in the DOM tree. If this sounds a little too technical for you, don't worry; just remember that XPath is the most powerful way to find a specific web control.

```
// clicking the check box under 'div2' container
driver.FindElement(By.XPath("//*[@id='div2']/input[@type='checkbox']")).
Click();
```

Some testers feel intimidated by the complexity of XPath. However, in practice, there is only a limited scope of XPath to master for testers.

AVOID USING COPIED XPATH FROM BROWSER'S DEVELOPER TOOL

Browser's Developer Tool (right-click to select Inspect Element) is very useful for identifying a web element in a web page. You can get the XPath of a web element there, as shown here (in Chrome):

This is the copied XPath for the second Click Here link in the example:

```
//*[@id="container"]/div[3]/div[2]/a
```

It works. However, I do not recommend this approach, as the test script is fragile. If the developer adds another div under <div id='container'>, the copied XPath is no longer correct for the element, although //div[contains(text(), "Second")]/a[text()="Click here"] still works.

In summary, XPath is a very powerful way to locate web elements when Id, Name, or LinkText are not applicable. Try to use an XPath expression that is less vulnerable to structure changes around the web element.

Find element by Tag Name

There are a limited set of tag names in HTML (https://developer.mozilla.org/en/docs/Web/HTML/Element). In other words, many elements share the same tag names on a web page. We normally don't use the tag_name locator by itself to locate an element. We often use it with others in a chained locator (see the section "Chain FindElement to find child elements" later in the chapter). However, there is an exception.

```
driver.FindElement(By.TagName("body")).Text;
```

This test statement returns the text view of a web page. This is very useful, as Selenium WebDriver does not have built-in method to return the text of a web page, commonly used for assertion.

Find element by Class

The class attribute of an HTML element is used for styling. It can also be used for identifying elements. Commonly, an HTML element's class attribute has multiple values, like shown here.

```
<a href="back.html" class="btn btn-default">Cancel</a>
<input type="submit" class="btn btn-deault btn-primary">Submit</input>
```

You could use any one of them.

```
driver.FindElement(By.ClassName("btn-primary")).Click(); // Submit button
driver.FindElement(By.ClassName("btn")).Click();    // Cancel link

// the below will return the error "Compound class names not permitted"
// driver.FindElement((By.ClassName("btn btn-deault btn-primary")).Click();
```

The ClassName locator is convenient for testing JavaScript/CSS libraries (e.g., TinyMCE) that typically use a set of defined class names.

```
// inline editing
driver.FindElement(By.Id("client_notes")).Click();
System.Threading.Thread.Sleep(500);
driver.FindElement(By.ClassName("editable-textarea")).SendKeys("inline notes");
System.Threading.Thread.Sleep(500);
driver.FindElement(By.ClassName("editable-submit")).Click();
```

Find element by CSS Selector

You can also use CSS Path to locate a web element.

```
driver.FindElement(By.CssSelector("#div2 > input[type='checkbox']")).Click();
```

However, the use of CSS Selector is generally more prone to structure changes of a web page.

Chain FindElement to find child elements

For a page containing more than one element with the same attributes, like the one shown here

```
<div id="div1">
  <input type="checkbox" name="same" value="on"> Same checkbox in Div 1
</div>
<div id="div2">
  <input type="checkbox" name="same" value="on"> Same checkbox in Div 2
</div>
```

we could use XPath locator.

```
driver.FindElement(By.XPath("//div[@id='div2']/input[@name='same']"))
```

here is another way: Chain FindElement to find a child element.

```
driver.FindElement(By.Id("div2")).FindElement(By.Name("same")).Click();
```

Find multiple elements

As its name suggests, FindElements returns a list of matched elements. Its syntax is exactly the same as FindElement; that is, it can use any of the eight locators.

The test statements below will find two check boxes under div#container and click the second one.

```
ReadOnlyCollection<IWebElement> checkbox_elems = driver.FindElements
(By.XPath("//div[@id='container']//input[@type='checkbox']"));
System.Console.WriteLine(checkbox_elems); // => 2
checkbox_elems[1].Click();
```

Sometimes FindElement fails due to multiple matching elements on a page that you were not aware of. FindElements will come in handy to find them out.

CHAPTER 3

Hyperlink

Hyperlinks (or links) are fundamental elements of web pages. As a matter of fact, it is hyperlinks that make the World Wide Web possible. A sample link is shown in Figure 3-1 provided, followed by the HTML source.

Recommend Selenium

Figure 3-1. *An example of a hyperlink*

HTML source

```
<a href="index.html" id="recommend_selenium_link" class="nav" data-id="123"
style="font-size: 14px;">Recommend Selenium</a>
```

Click a link by text

Using text is probably the most direct way to click a link in Selenium, as it is what we see on the page.

```
driver.FindElement(By.LinkText("Recommend Selenium")).Click();
```

Click a link by ID

```
driver.FindElement(By.Id("recommend_selenium_link")).Click();
```

Furthermore, if you are testing a web site with multiple languages, using IDs is probably the only feasible option. You do not want to write test scripts like this:

```
// IsItalian()) and IsChinese() helper methods, defined elsewhere
if (IsItalian()) {   // a helper function determines the locale
driver.FindElement(By.LinkText("Accedi")).Click();
} else if (IsChinese()) {
```

```
  driver.FindElement(By.LinkText, "登录").Click();
} else {
  driver.FindElement(By.LinkText("Sign in")).Click();
}
```

Click a link by partial text

```
driver.FindElement(By.PartialLinkText("Recommend Seleni")).Click();
```

Click a link by XPath

The following example is finding a link with the text 'Recommend Selenium' under a
<p> tag.

```
driver.FindElement(By.XPath("//p/a[text()='Recommend Selenium']")).Click();
```

You might say the former example (find by LinkText) is simpler and more intuitive,
and that's correct, but let's examine another example, shown in Figure 3-2.

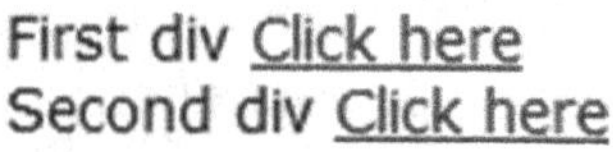

First div Click here
Second div Click here

Figure 3-2. A hyperlinks example

On this page, there are two Click Here links.

HTML source

```
<div>
  First div
  <a href="link-url.html">Click here</a>
</div>
<div>
  Second div
  <a href="link-partial.html">Click here</a>
</div>
```

If the test case requires you to click the second Click Here link, the simple

```
FindElement(By.LinkText("Click here"))
```

won't work (as it clicks the first one). Here is a way to accomplish this using XPath:

```
driver.FindElement(By.XPath("//div[contains(text(),
\"Second\")]/a[text()=\"Click here\"]")).Click();
```

Click nth link with exact same label

It is not uncommon that there is more than one link with exactly the same text. By default, Selenium will choose the first one. What if you want to click the second or nth one?

The web page shown in Figure 3-3 contains three Show Answer links.

1. Do you think automated testing is important and valuable? Show Answer

2. Why didn't you do automated testing in your projects previously? Show Answer

3. Your project now has so comprehensive automated test suite, What changed? Show Answer

Figure 3-3. *Three links with the same label*

To click the second one, use the following code.

```
Assert.IsTrue(driver.FindElements(By.LinkText("Show Answer")).Count == 2);
ReadOnlyCollection<IWebElement> links = driver.FindElements
(By.LinkText("Show Answer"));
links[1].Click(); // click the second one
Assert.IsTrue(driver.PageSource.Contains("second link page"));
// second link
```

FindElements returns a collection (also called an array by some) of web controls matching the criteria in appearing order. Selenium (in fact C#) uses 0-based indexing; that is, the first one is 0.

Click nth link by CSS selector

You can also use CSS selector to locate a web element.

```
// Click the 3rd link directly in <p> tag
driver.FindElement(By.CssSelector("p > a:nth-child(3)")).Click();
```

However, generally speaking, the use of a stylesheet is more prone to changes.

Verify that a link is present or not

```
Assert.IsTrue(driver.FindElement(By.LinkText("Recommend Selenium")).
Displayed);
Assert.IsTrue(driver.FindElement(By.Id("recommend_selenium_link")).
Displayed);
```

Getting link data attributes

Once a web control is identified, we can get the other attributes of the element. This is generally applicable to most of the controls.

```
Assert.AreEqual(TestHelper.SiteUrl() + "/index.html",  driver.
FindElement(By.LinkText("Recommend Selenium")).GetAttribute("href") );
Assert.AreEqual("recommend_selenium_link", driver.FindElement(By.
LinkText("Recommend Selenium")).GetAttribute("id"));
Assert.AreEqual("Recommend Selenium", driver.FindElement(By.Id("recommend_
selenium_link")).Text);
Assert.AreEqual("a", driver.FindElement(By.Id("recommend_selenium_link")).
TagName);
```

You can also get the value of custom attributes of this element and its inline CSS style.

```
Assert.AreEqual("font-size: 14px;", driver.FindElement(By.Id("recommend_
selenium_link")).GetAttribute("style"));
// Please note using attribute_value("style") won't work
Assert.AreEqual("123", driver.FindElement(By.Id("recommend_selenium_link")).
GetAttribute("data-id"));
```

Test links open a new browser window

Clicking the following link will open the linked URL in a new browser window or tab.

```
<a href="http://testwisely.com/demo" target="_blank">Open new window</a>
```

Although we could use the SwitchTo() method to find the new browser window.

```
driver.FindElement(By.LinkText("Open new window")).Click();
driver.SwitchTo().Window(driver.WindowHandles[1]); # change window
driver.FindElement(By.Name("name")).SendKeys("on new window");
driver.Close();
driver.SwitchTo().Window(driver.WindowHandles[0]);  // back
driver.FindElement(By.LinkText("Recommend Selenium")).Click();
```

However it will be easier to perform all testing within one browser window. Here is how:

```
String currentUrl = driver.Url;
String newWindowUrl = driver.FindElement(By.LinkText("Open new window")).
GetAttribute("href");
driver.Navigate().GoToUrl(newWindowUrl);
driver.FindElement(By.Name("name")).SendKeys("sometext");
driver.Navigate().GoToUrl(currentUrl); // back
```

In this test script, we use a local variable currentUrl to store the current URL.

CHAPTER 4

Button

Buttons come in two forms: standard and submit buttons, as shown in Figure 4-1. Standard buttons are usually created by the 'button' tag, whereas submit buttons are created by the 'input' tag (normally within form controls).

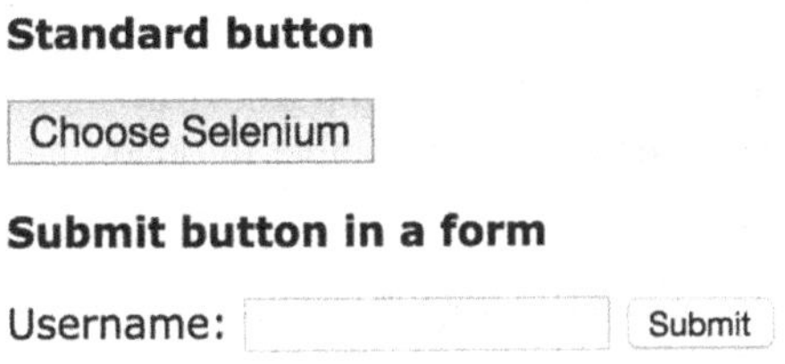

Standard button

Choose Selenium

Submit button in a form

Username: [   ] Submit

Figure 4-1. *Examples of standard and submit buttons*

HTML source

```
<button id="choose_selenium_btn" class="nav" data-id="123" style="font-size:
14px;">Choose Selenium</button>
<!-- ... -->
<form name="input" action="index.html" method="get">
  Username: <input type="text" name="user">
  <input type="submit" name="submit_action" value="Submit">
</form>
```

Note that some controls look like buttons, but are actually hyperlinks by CSS styling.

Click a button by text

```
driver.FindElement(By.XPath("//button[contains(text(),
'Choose Selenium')]")).Click();
```

Click a form button by text

For an input button (in a HTML input tag) in a form, the text shown on the button is the 'value' attribute, which might contain extra spaces or invisible characters.

```
<input type="submit" name="submit_action" value="Space After "/>
```

The following test script will fail, as there is a space character in the end.

```
driver.FindElement(By.XPath("//input[@value='Space After']")).Click();
```

Changing to match the value exactly will fix it.

```
driver.FindElement(By.XPath("//input[@value='Space After ']")).Click();
```

Submit a form

In the official Selenium tutorial, the operation of clicking a submit button is done by calling the Submit function on an input element within a form. For example, the following test script is to test user sign in.

```
IWebElement username_element = driver.FindElement(By.Name("user"));
username_element.SendKeys("agileway");
IWebElement password_element = driver.FindElement(By.Name("password"));
password_element.SendKeys("secret");
username_element.Submit();
```

However, this is not my preferred approach. Whenever possible, I write test scripts this way: One test step corresponds to one user operation, such as a text entry or a mouse click. This helps me to identify issues quicker during test debugging. Using Submit means testers need a step to define a variable to store an identified element (line 1 in the preceding test script). To me, it breaks the flow. Here is my version:

```
driver.FindElement(By.Name("user")).SendKeys("agileway");
driver.FindElement(By.Name("password")).SendKeys("secret");
driver.FindElement(By.XPath("//input[@value='Sign in']")).Click();
```

Furthermore, if there is more than one submit button (unlikely but possible) in a form, calling Submit is equivalent to clicking the first submit button only, which might cause confusion.

Click a button by ID

As always, a better way to identify a button is to use IDs. This applies to all controls if there are IDs present.

```
driver.FindElement(By.Id("choose_selenium_btn")).Click();
```

For testers who work with the development team, rather than spending hours finding a way to identify a web control, just go to programmers and ask them to add IDs. It usually takes very little effort for them to do so.

Click a button by name

In an input button, we can use a new generic attribute name to locate a control.

```
driver.FindElement(By.Name("submit_action")).Click();
```

Click an image button

There is also another type of button: an image that works like a submit button in a form, like the one shown in Figure 4-2.

```
<input type="image" src="images/button_go.jpg"/>
```

Go →

Figure 4-2. *An example of an image button*

Besides using an ID, the button can also be identified by using the `src` attribute.

```
driver.FindElement(By.XPath("//input[contains(@src, 'button_go.jpg')]")).
Click();
```

Click a button via JavaScript

You can also invoke clicking a button via JavaScript. I had a case where normal approaches didn't click a button reliably on Firefox, but this JavaScript method worked well.

```
IWebElement aBtn = driver.FindElement(By.Id("choose_selenium_btn"));
((IJavaScriptExecutor)driver).ExecuteScript("arguments[0].click();", aBtn);
```

Assert a button present

Just like hyperlinks, we can use Displayed to check whether a control is present on a web page. This check applies to most of the web controls in Selenium.

```
Assert.IsTrue(driver.FindElement(By.Id("choose_selenium_btn")).Displayed);
driver.FindElement(By.LinkText("Hide")).Click();
System.Threading.Thread.Sleep(500);
Assert.IsFalse(driver.FindElement(By.Id("choose_selenium_btn")).Displayed);
```

Assert a button enabled or disabled

A web control can be in a disabled state. A disabled button is unable to be clicked, and it is displayed differently (see Figure 4-3).

```
Normally enabling or disabling buttons (or other web controls) is triggered
by JavaScripts.Assert.IsTrue(driver.FindElement(By.Id("choose_selenium_
btn")).Enabled);
driver.FindElement(By.LinkText("Disable")).Click();
System.Threading.Thread.Sleep(500); Assert.IsFalse(driver.FindElement
(By.Id("choose_selenium_btn")).Enabled);
driver.FindElement(By.LinkText("Enable")).Click();
System.Threading.Thread.Sleep(500);
Assert.IsTrue(driver.FindElement(By.Id("choose_selenium_btn")).Enabled);
```

| Choose Selenium |

Figure 4-3. *An example of a disabled button*

In the preceding example, the change of the button's state is set by invoking an operation on the page. You may also do that from test script by calling JavaScript directly.

```
IWebElement aBtn = driver.FindElement(By.Id("choose_selenium_btn"));
Assert.IsTrue(aBtn.Enabled);
((IJavaScriptExecutor)driver).ExecuteScript("arguments[0].disabled = true;",
aBtn); Assert.IsFalse(driver.FindElement(By.Id("choose_selenium_btn")).
Enabled);
((IJavaScriptExecutor)driver).ExecuteScript("arguments[0].disabled =
false;", aBtn); Assert.IsTrue(driver.FindElement(By.Id("choose_selenium_
btn")).Enabled)
```

■ ■ ■

CHAPTER 5

TextField and TextArea

Text fields are commonly used in a form to pass user-entered text data to the server. There are two variants (prior to HTML5): password fields and text areas. The characters in password fields are masked (shown as asterisks or circles). Text areas allow multiple lines of text. These variants are shown in Figure 5-1.

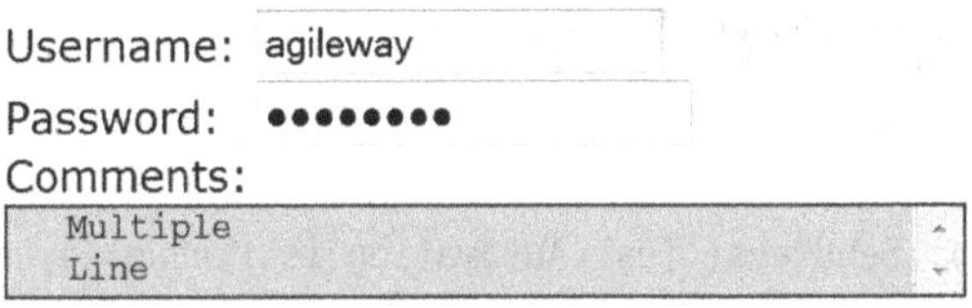

Username: agileway
Password: ••••••••
Comments:
```
Multiple
Line
```

Figure 5-1. *Password field and text areas*

HTML source

```
Username: <input type="text" name="username" id="user"><br>
Password: <input type="password" name="password" id="pass"> <br/>
Comments: <br/>
<textarea id="comments" rows="2" cols="60" name="comments"></textarea>
```

Enter Text into a Text Field by Name

The name attribute is the identification used by programmers to process data. It applies to all the web controls in a standard web form.

```
driver.FindElement(By.Name("username")).SendKeys("agileway");
```

Enter Text into a Text Field by ID

```
driver.FindElement(By.Id("user")).SendKeys("agileway");
```

Enter Text into a Password Field

In Selenium, password text fields are treated as normal text fields, except that the entered text is masked.

```
driver.FindElement(By.Id("pass")).SendKeys("testisfun");
```

Clear a Text Field

Calling SendKeys() to the same text field will concatenate the new text with the old text. It is therefore a good idea to clear a text field first, then send keys to it.

```
driver.FindElement(By.Name("username")).SendKeys("test");
driver.FindElement(By.Name("username")).SendKeys(" wisely"); // test wisely
driver.FindElement(By.Name("username")).Clear();
driver.FindElement(By.Name("username")).SendKeys("agileway");
```

Enter Text into a Multiline Text Area

Selenium treats text areas the same as text fields.

```
driver.FindElement(By.Id("comments")).SendKeys("Test Automation is\r\nFun!");
```

The \r\n represents a new line.

Assert Value

```
driver.FindElement(By.Id("user")).SendKeys("testwisely");
Assert.AreEqual("testwisely", driver.FindElement(By.Id("user")).
GetAttribute("value"));
```

Focus on a Control

Once we identify one control, we can set the focus on it. There is no focus function on elements in Selenium, but we can focus a control by sending empty keystrokes to it.

```
driver.FindElement(By.Id("pass")).SendKeys("");
```

Alternatively, you can use JavaScript.

```
IWebElement elem = driver.FindElement(By.Id("pass"));
((IJavaScriptExecutor)driver).ExecuteScript("arguments[0].focus();", elem);
```

This workaround can be quite useful. When testing a long web page with some controls that are not visible, trying to click them might throw an Element Is Not Visible error. In that case, setting the focus on the element might make it visible.

Set a Value to a Read-only or Disabled Text Field

Read-only and disabled text fields are not editable and are shown differently in the browser (typically grayed out).

```
Read only text field:
<input type="text" name="readonly_text" readonly="true"/> <br/>
Disabled text field:
<input type="text" name="disabled_text" disabled="true"/>
```

If a text box is set to be read-only, the following test step will not work.

```
driver.FindElement(By.Name("readonly_text")).SendKeys("new value");
```

Here is a workaround:

```
((IJavaScriptExecutor)driver).ExecuteScript("$('#readonly_text').val('bypass');");
Assert.AreEqual("bypass", driver.FindElement(By.Id("readonly_text")).
GetAttribute("value"));
((IJavaScriptExecutor)driver).ExecuteScript("$('#disabled_text').val('anyuse');");
```

Figure 5-2 is a screenshot of disabled and read-only text fields that were "injected" with two values by the preceding test script.

Disabled text field: anyuse

Readonly text field: bypass

Figure 5-2. *Disabled and read-only text fields*

Set and assert the value of a hidden field

A hidden field is often used to store a default value.

```
<input type="hidden" name="currency" value="USD"/>
```

The following test script asserts the value of the preceding hidden field and changes its value using JavaScript.

```
IWebElement theHiddenElem = driver.FindElement(By.Name("currency"));
Assert.AreEqual("USD", theHiddenElem.GetAttribute("value"));
((IJavaScriptExecutor)driver).ExecuteScript("arguments[0].value='AUD';",
theHiddenElem);
Assert.AreEqual("AUD", theHiddenElem.GetAttribute("value"));
```

37

■ ■ ■

CHAPTER 6

Radio Button

Radio buttons are commonly used interface features. Figure 6-1 shows a simple example.

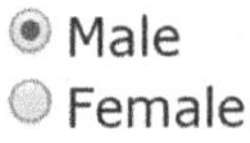

⦿ Male
◯ Female

Figure 6-1. *An example of radio buttons*

HTML source

```
<input type="radio" name="gender" value="male" id="radio_male"
checked="true">Male<br>
<input type="radio" name="gender" value="female" id="radio_female">Female
```

Select a Radio Button

The radio buttons in the same radio group have the same name. To click one radio option, the value needs to be specified. Please note that the value is not the text shown next to the radio button (i.e., the label). To find out the value of a radio button, inspect the HTML source.

```
driver.FindElement(By.XPath("//input[@name='gender' and @value='female']")).
Click();
System.Threading.Thread.Sleep(500);
driver.FindElement(By.XPath("//input[@name='gender' and @value='male']")).Click();
```

As always, if there are IDs, using Id finder is easier.

```
driver.FindElement(By.Id("radio_female")).Click();
```

Clear Radio Option Selection

It is fine to click a radio button that is currently selected; however, it will not have any effect.

```
driver.FindElement(By.Id("radio_female")).Click();
driver.FindElement(By.Id("radio_female")).Click(); // already selected, no effect
```

Once a radio button is selected, the way to clear it in Selenium (or in practical use) is to select another radio button (Watir, another test framework, can clear a radio button selection). The following test script below will throw an error: "Invalid Element State: Element Must Be User-Editable in Order to Clear It."

```
driver.FindElement(By.XPath("//input[@name='gender' and @value='female']")).
Click();
try
{
    driver.FindElement(By.XPath("//input[@name='gender' and
@value='female']")).Clear();
}
catch (Exception ex)
{
    // Selenium does not allow
    Console.WriteLine("Selenium does not allow clear currently selected
    radio button, just select another one");
    driver.FindElement(By.XPath("//input[@name='gender' and
    @value='male']")).Click();
}
```

Assert a Radio Option is Selected

```
driver.FindElement(By.XPath("//input[@name='gender' and @value='female']")).
Click();
Assert.IsTrue(driver.FindElement(By.XPath("//input[@name='gender' and
@value='female']")).Selected);
Assert.IsFalse(driver.FindElement(By.XPath("//input[@name='gender' and
@value='male']")).Selected);
```

Iterate Radio Buttons in a Radio Group

So far we have been focusing on identifying web controls by using one type of locator, FindElement. Here I introduce another type of locator (I call them plural locators): FindElements.

```
Assert.AreEqual(2, driver.FindElements(By.Name("gender")).Count);

foreach (IWebElement rb in driver.FindElements(By.Name("gender")))
{
    if (rb.GetAttribute("value").Equals("female"))
    {
        rb.Click();
    }
}
```

Different from FindElement, which returns one matched control, FindElements returns a list of them (also known as an array). This can be quite handy, especially when controls are hard to locate.

Click nth Radio Button in a Group

Once I was testing an online calendar, there were many time slots, and the HTML for each of these time slots was exactly the same. I simply identified the time slot by using the index (as shown here) on one of these "plural" locators.

```
driver.FindElements(By.Name("gender"))[1].Click();
Assert.IsTrue(driver.FindElement(By.XPath("//input[@name='gender' and @
value='female']")).Selected);

driver.FindElements(By.Name("gender"))[0].Click();
Assert.IsTrue(driver.FindElement(By.XPath("//input[@name='gender' and @
value='male']")).Selected);
```

Click Radio Button by the Following Label

Some .NET controls generate poor quality HTML fragments like the one shown here.

```
<div id="q1" class="question">
  <div class="question-answer col-lg-5">
    <div class="yes-no">
      <input id="QuestionViewModels_1__SelectedAnswerId"
      name="QuestionViewModels[1].SelectedAnswerId" type="radio"
      value="c225306e-8d8e-45b0-8261-22617d9796b5">
      <label for="QuestionViewModels_1__SelectedAnswerId">Yes</label>
    </div>
```

```
<div class="yes-no">
  <input id="QuestionViewModels_1__SelectedAnswerId"
  name="QuestionViewModels[1].SelectedAnswerId" type="radio"
  value="85ff8db7-1c58-47a2-a978-581200fb7098">
  <label for="QuestionViewModels_1__SelectedAnswerId">No</label>
</div>
  </div>
</div>
```

The id attributes of the preceding two radio buttons are the same, and the values are meaningless to humans. The only thing that can be used to identify a radio button is the text in label elements. The solution is to use XPath locator. You might have noticed that input (radio button) and label are siblings in the HTML DOM tree. We can use this relation to come up with an XPath that identifies the label text, then the radio button.

```
IWebElement elem = driver.FindElement(By.XPath("//div[@id='q1']//
label[contains(.,'Yes')]/../input[@type='radio']"));
elem.Click();
```

Please note the use of /../ in the preceding XPath. When the target element is difficult to identify but one of its sibling elements is available, use this trick.

Customized Radio Buttons: iCheck

There are a number of plug-ins that customize radio buttons into a more stylish form, like the one shown in Figure 6-2 (using iCheck).

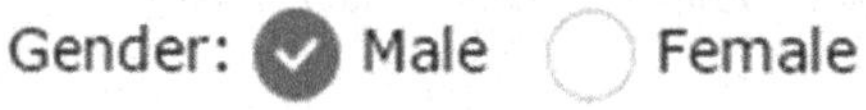

Gender: ✅ Male ⭕ Female

Figure 6-2. *A stylized radio button using iCheck*

The iCheck JavaScript transforms the radio button HTML fragment

```
<input type="radio" name="sex" id="q2_1" value="male"> Male
```

into

```
<div class="iradio_square-red" style="position: relative;">
  <input type="radio" name="sex" id="q2_1" value="male" style="....
  <ins class="iCheck-helper" style="...
</div>
```

Here are test scripts to drive iCheck radio buttons.

```
// Error: Element is not clickable
// driver.FindElement(By.Id("q2_1")).click();
driver.FindElements(By.ClassName("iradio_square-red"))[0].Click();
driver.FindElements(By.ClassName("iradio_square-red"))[1].Click();

// More precise with XPath

driver.FindElement(By.XPath("//div[contains(@class, 'iradio_square-red')]/
input[@type='radio' and @value='male']/../ins")).Click();
```

■ ■ ■

CHAPTER 7

Check Box

Check boxes are common elements in user interfaces. An example is shown in Figure 7-1.

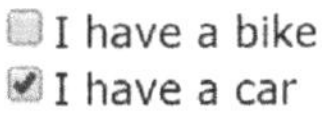

☐ I have a bike
☑ I have a car

Figure 7-1. *An example of check boxes*

HTML source

```
<input type="checkbox" name="vehicle_bike" value="on" id="checkbox_bike">I
have a bike<br>
<input type="checkbox" name="vehicle_car" id="checkbox_car">I have a car
```

Check by name

```
driver.FindElement(By.Name("vehicle_bike")).Click();
```

Check by ID

Clicking a check box, in fact, is a toggle: The first click selects the check box and the next one clears it. The following test statements make sure a check is a check.

```
IWebElement the_checkbox = driver.FindElement(By.Id("checkbox_car"));
if (!the_checkbox.Selected)

    {

    the_checkbox.Click();

    }
```

Clear a check box

```
IWebElement the_checkbox = driver.FindElement(By.Name("vehicle_bike"));
the_checkbox.Click();
// can't use Clear() that works for textfields
if (the_checkbox.Selected)

    {

    the_checkbox.Click();

    }
```

Assert a check box is checked (or not)

```
IWebElement the_checkbox = driver.FindElement(By.Name("vehicle_bike"));
Assert.IsFalse(the_checkbox.Selected);
the_checkbox.Click();
Assert.IsTrue(the_checkbox.Selected);
```

Chain FindElement to find child elements

We could use XPath locator (see Chapter 2) to identify elements with same attributes, as shown here.

```
<div id="div1">
  <input type="checkbox" name="same" value="on"> Same checkbox in Div 1
</div>
<div id="div2">
  <input type="checkbox" name="same" value="on"> Same checkbox in Div 2
</div>
```

Here is another way: Chain FindElement to find a child element.

```
driver.FindElement(By.Id("div2")).FindElement(By.Name("same")).Click();
```

Customized Check Boxes: iCheck

There are a number of plug-ins that customize check boxes into a more stylish form, like the one shown in Figure 7-2 using iCheck.

Figure 7-2. *An example of a stylized check box*

The iCheck JavaScript transforms the check box HTML fragment

```
<input type="checkbox" name="sports[]" value="Soccer">  Soccer <br/>
```

to

```
<div class="icheckbox_square-red" style="position: relative;">
    <input type="checkbox" name="sports[]" value="Soccer" style="....
    <ins class="iCheck-helper" style="…
</div>
```

Here are test scripts to drive iCheck check boxes.

```
driver.FindElements(By.ClassName("icheckbox_square-red"))[0].Click();
driver.FindElements(By.ClassName("icheckbox_square-red"))[1].Click(); //2nd

// More precise with XPath

    driver.FindElement(By.XPath("//div[contains(@class, 'icheckbox_square-
red')]/input[@type='checkbox' and @value='Soccer']/..")).Click();
```

■ ■ ■

CHAPTER 8

Select List

A select list is also known as a drop-down list or combo box. An example is shown in Figure 8-1.

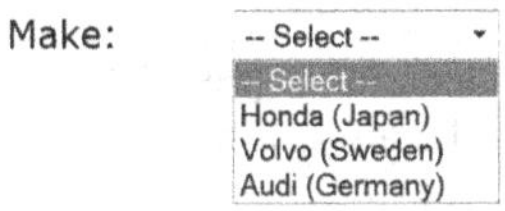

Make: -- Select --   ▾
        -- Select --
        Honda (Japan)
        Volvo (Sweden)
        Audi (Germany)

Figure 8-1. *An example of a select list*

HTML source

```
<select name="car_make" id="car_make_select">
  <option value="">-- Select --</option>
  <option value="honda">Honda (Japan)</option>
  <option value="volvo">Volvo (Sweden)</option>
  <option value="audi">Audi (Germany)</option>
</select>
```

Select an option by text

The label of a select list is what we can see in the browser.

```
IWebElement elem = driver.FindElement(By.Name("car_make"));
SelectElement select = new SelectElement(elem);
select.SelectByText("Volvo (Sweden)");
```

The standard Selenium class name for Select Lists is Select (that is how is called in Java). As Select is a reserved keyword in C#, the class is named SelectElement for Selenium C# binding.

You may also replace the three preceding test statements with one.

```
new SelectElement(driver.FindElement(By.Name("car_make"))).
SelectByText("Honda (Japan)");
```

Select an option by value

The value of a select list is what is to be passed to the server.

```
IWebElement elem = driver.FindElement(By.Id("car_make_select"));
SelectElement select = new SelectElement(elem);
select.SelectByValue("audi");
```

Select an option by index

Sometimes, we don't care about an exact option, we just need to select one to pass the validation. In that case, then by index is a better way, especially for dynamic options.

```
IWebElement elem = driver.FindElement(By.Id("car_make_select"));
SelectElement select = new SelectElement(elem);
select.SelectByIndex(1); // 0 based index
```

Select an option by iterating all options

Here I show you a far more complex way to select an option in a select list, not for the sake of complexity, of course. A select list contains options, where each option itself is a valid control in Selenium.

```
IWebElement selectElem = driver.FindElement(By.Id("car_make_select"));
foreach (IWebElement option in selectElem.FindElements(By.TagName("option")))

{
    if (option.Text.Equals("Volvo (Sweden)"))
    {
        option.Click();
    }
}
```

Select multiple options

A select list also supports multiple selections, as displayed in Figure 8-2.

Framework:

Figure 8-2. *A select list with multiple selections*

HTML source

```
<select id="framework_select" name="test_framework" multiple="multiple">
  <option></option>
  <option value="rwebspec">RWebSpec</option>
  <option value="watir">Watir</option>
  <option value="selenium">Selenium</option>
</select>
```

Test script

```
IWebElement elem = driver.FindElement(By.Name("test_framework"));
SelectElement select = new SelectElement(elem);
select.SelectByText("Selenium");
select.SelectByValue("rwebspec");
select.SelectByIndex(2);
Assert.AreEqual(3, select.AllSelectedOptions.Count);
```

Clear one selection

```
IWebElement elem = driver.FindElement(By.Name("test_framework"));
SelectElement select = new SelectElement(elem);
select.SelectByText("RWebSpec");
select.SelectByText("Selenium");
select.SelectByText("Watir");
select.DeselectByText("RWebSpec");
select.DeselectByValue("selenium");
select.DeselectByIndex(0);
Assert.AreEqual(0, select.AllSelectedOptions.Count);
```

51

Clear all selections

Clearing a selection works the same way for both single and multiple select lists.

```
IWebElement elem = driver.FindElement(By.Name("test_framework"));
SelectElement select = new SelectElement(elem);
select.SelectByText("Selenium");
select.SelectByText("RWebSpec");
select.DeselectAll();
Assert.IsTrue(select.AllSelectedOptions.Count == 0 );
```

Assert selected option

To verify a particular option is currently selected in a select list, use this code.

```
IWebElement elem = driver.FindElement(By.Id("car_make_select"));
SelectElement select = new SelectElement(elem);
select.SelectByValue("audi");
Assert.AreEqual("Audi (Germany)", select.SelectedOption.Text);
```

Assert the value of a select list

Here is another quick and simple way to check the current selected value of a select list:

```
IWebElement elem = driver.FindElement(By.Id("car_make_select"));
SelectElement select = new SelectElement(elem);
select.SelectByText("Volvo (Sweden)");
Assert.AreEqual("volvo", select.SelectedOption.GetAttribute("value"));
```

Assert multiple selections

A multiple select list can have multiple options selected.

```
IWebElement elem = driver.FindElement(By.Name("test_framework"));
SelectElement select = new SelectElement(elem);
select.SelectByText("Selenium");
select.SelectByText("RWebSpec");

IList<IWebElement> selected = select.AllSelectedOptions;
Assert.AreEqual(2, selected.Count);
Assert.AreEqual("RWebSpec", selected[0].Text); // display order
Assert.AreEqual("Selenium", selected[1].Text);
```

Note that, even though the test script selected "Selenium" first, when it comes to assertion, the first selected option is "RWebSpec", not "Selenium".

■ ■ ■

CHAPTER 9

Navigation and Browser

Driving common web controls were covered in Chapters 2 through 8. In this chapter, I show how to manage browser windows and page navigation in them.

Go to a URL

```
driver.Navigate().GoToUrl("https://google.com");
```

Alternatively, set the `driver.Url` property.

```
driver.Url = "http://testwisely.com";
```

Visit pages within a site

`driver.Navigate().GoToUrl()` takes a full URL. Most of time, testers test against a single site and specifying a full URL (e.g., `http://...`) is not necessary. We can create a reusable function to simplify its usage.

```
String siteRootUrl = "http://test.testwisely.com";

// ...

public void Visit(String path) {
    driver.Navigate().GoToUrl(siteRootUrl + path);
}

[TestMethod]
public void TestGoToPageWithinSiteUsingFunction() {
    Visit("/demo");
    Visit("/demo/survey");
    Visit("/");      // home page
}
```

Apart from being more readable, there is another benefit with this approach. If you want to run the same test against a different server (the same application deployed on another machine), you only need to make one change: the value of siteRootUrl.

```
String siteRootUrl = "http://dev.testwisely.com";
```

Perform actions from the right-click context menu

Operations with the right-click context menu are commonly page navigations, such as Back to Previous Page. We can achieve the same by calling the test framework's navigation operations directly.

```
driver.Navigate().Back();
driver.Navigate().Refresh();
driver.Navigate().Forward();
```

Open browser in certain size

Many modern web sites use responsive web design; that is, page content layout changes depending on the browser window size. This does increase testing effort, which means testers need to test web sites in different browser window sizes. Fortunately, Selenium has a convenient way to resize the browser window.

```
driver.Manage().Window.Size = new System.Drawing.Size(1024, 768);
```

Maximize browser window

```
driver.Manage().Window.Maximize();
System.Threading.Thread.Sleep(1000);  // wait 1 second to see the effect
driver.Manage().Window.Size = new System.Drawing.Size(1024, 768);
```

Move browser window

We can move the browser window (started by the test script) to a certain position on screen, with (0, 0) being the top left of the screen. The position of the browser's window won't affect the test results. This might be useful for utility applications; for example, a background video program can capture a certain area on the screen.

```
driver.Manage().Window.Position = new System.Drawing.Point(100, 100);
System.Threading.Thread.Sleep(1000);
driver.Manage().Window.Position = new System.Drawing.Point(0, 0);
```

Minimize browser window

Surprisingly, there is no minimize window function in Selenium. The following hack achieves the same result.

```
driver.Manage().Window.Position = new System.Drawing.Point(-2000, 0);
driver.FindElement(By.LinkText("Hyperlink")).Click();
System.Threading.Thread.Sleep(2000);
driver.Manage().Window.Position = new System.Drawing.Point(0, 0);
```

The test execution still can run while the browser's window is minimized.

Scroll focus to control

For certain controls that are not viewable in a web page (due to JavaScript), WebDriver enables a user to click on them by returning an error like Element Is Not Clickable at Point (1180, 43). The solution is to scroll the browser view to the control.

```
IWebElement elem = driver.FindElement(By.Name("submit_action_2"));
int elemPos = elem.Location.Y;
((IJavaScriptExecutor)driver).ExecuteScript("window.scroll(0, " + elemPos + ");");
elem.Click();
```

Switch between browser windows or tabs

A "target='_blank'" hyperlink opens a page in another browser window or tab (depending on the browser setting). Selenium drives the browser within a scope of one browser window. However, we can use Selenium's SwitchTo function to change the target browser.

```
driver.FindElement(By.LinkText("Hyperlink")).Click();
driver.FindElement(By.LinkText("Open new window")).Click();
ReadOnlyCollection<String> windowHandles = driver.WindowHandles;
String firstTab = (String) windowHandles[0];
String lastTab = windowHandles[windowHandles.Count - 1] ;
driver.SwitchTo().Window(lastTab);
Assert.IsTrue(driver.FindElement(By.TagName("body")).Text.Contains("This is
url link page"));
driver.SwitchTo().Window(firstTab); // back to first tab/window
Assert.IsTrue(driver.FindElement(By.LinkText("Open new window")).Displayed);
```

Remember current web page URL and return to it later

We can store the page's URL into an instance variable (e.g., url).

```
String url; // instance variable

[TestInitialize]
public void Before() {
   url = driver.Url;
}

//...

[TestMethod]
public void TestSelectOptionByLabel() {
   driver.FindElement(By.LinkText("Button")).Click();
   //...
   driver.Navigate().GoToUrl(url);
}
```

   In previous recipes, I used local variables to remember some value, and use it later. A local variable only works in its local scope, typically within one test case (in our context, or more specifically between public void TestXXX() { to }).

   In this example, the url variable is used in the [TestInitialize] scope. To make it accessible to the test cases in the test script file, I define it as an instance variable url.

■ ■ ■

CHAPTER 10

Assertion

Without assertions, often known as checks, a test script is incomplete. Common assertions for testing web applications are the following:

- Page title (equals)
- Page text (contains or does not contain)
- Page source (contains or does not contain)
- Input element value (equals)
- Display element text (equals)
- Element state (selected, disabled, displayed)

Assert page title

```
Assert.AreEqual("TestWise IDE", driver.Title);
```

Assert page text

Figure 10-1 shows an example web page.

```
Text assertion with a  (tab before), and
(new line before)!
```

Figure 10-1. *An example web page*

HTML source

```
<PRE>Text assertion with a  (<b>tab</b> before), and
(new line before)!</PRE>
```

Test script

```
String matching_str = "Text assertion with a  (tab before), and \n(new line
before)!";
Assert.IsTrue(driver.FindElement(By.TagName("body")).Text.Contains(matching_str));
```

Note that the `driver.FindElement(By.TagName("body")).Text` returns the text view of a web page after stripping off the HTML tags, but might not be exactly the same as we saw in the browser.

Assert page source

The page source is raw HTML returned from the server.

```
String html_fragment = "Text assertion with a  (<b>tab</b> before), and
\n(new line before)!";
Assert.IsTrue(driver.PageSource.Contains(html_fragment));
```

Assert checkbox selected

```
Assert.IsTrue(driver.FindElement(By.Name("is_vip")).Selected);
```

Assert button enabled

```
Assert.IsTrue(driver.FindElement(By.Id("continue_btn")).Enabled);
```

Assert label text

HTML source

```
<label id="receipt_number">NB123454</label>
```

Label tags are commonly used in web pages to wrap some text. It can be quite useful to assert specific text.

```
Assert.AreEqual("First Label", driver.FindElement(By.Id("label_1")).Text);
```

Assert span text

HTML source

```
<span id="span_2">Second Span</span>
```

From testing perspectives, spans are the same as labels, just with a different tag name.

```
Assert.AreEqual("Second Span", driver.FindElement(By.Id("span_2")).Text);
```

Assert div text or HTML

Figure 10-2 shows an example page.

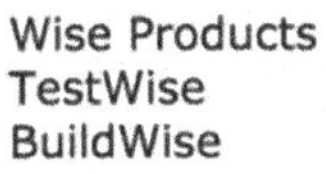

```
Wise Products
TestWise
BuildWise
```

Figure 10-2. *An example page*

HTML source

```
<div id="div_parent">
   Wise Products
   <div id="div_child_1">
     TestWise
   </div>
   <div id="div_child_2">
     BuildWise
   </div>
 </div>
```

Test script

```
Assert.AreEqual("TestWise", driver.FindElement(By.Id("div_child_1")).Text);
Assert.AreEqual("Wise Products\r\nTestWise\r\nBuildWise", driver.
FindElement(By.Id("div_parent")).Text);
```

Assert table text

HTML tables are commonly used for displaying grid data on web pages. Figure 10-3 shows an example page.

A	B
a	b

Figure 10-3. *An example page with table text*

HTML source

```
<table id="aha_table" cellpadding="1" border="1" width="30%">
  <tr id="row_1">
    <td id="cell_1_1">A</td>
    <td id="cell_1_2">B</td>
  </tr>
  <tr id="row_2">
    <td id="cell_2_1">a</td>
    <td id="cell_2_2">b</td>
  </tr>
</table>
```

Test script

```
IWebElement the_element = driver.FindElement(By.Id("alpha_table"));
Assert.AreEqual("A B\r\na b", the_element.Text);
Object html = ((IJavaScriptExecutor)driver).ExecuteScript("return
arguments[0].outerHTML;", the_element);
String htmlStr = (String)html;
Assert.IsTrue(htmlStr.Contains("<td id=\"cell_1_1\">A</td>"));
```

Assert text in a table cell

If a table cell (td tag) has a unique ID, it is easy.

```
Assert.AreEqual("A", driver.FindElement(By.Id("cell_1_1")).Text);
```

An alternative approach is to identify a table cell using row and column indexes (both starting with 1).

```
Assert.AreEqual("b", driver.FindElement(By.XPath("//table/tbody/tr[2]/
td[2]")).Text);
```

Assert text in a table row

```
Assert.AreEqual("A B", driver.FindElement(By.Id("row_1")).Text);
```

Assert image present

```
Assert.IsTrue(driver.FindElement(By.Id("next_go")).Displayed);
```

■ ■ ■

CHAPTER 11

Frames

HTML frames are treated as independent pages, which is not a good web design practice. As a result, few new sites use frames nowadays. However, there are quite a number of sites that use iframes.

Testing Frames

Figure 11-1 shows a fairly common frame layout: navigations on the top, menus on the left, and the main content on the right.

Figure 11-1. *A common frame layout*

HTML source

```
<frameset rows="100,*" frameborder="0" border="0" framespacing="0">
  <frame name="topNav" src="top_nav.html">
  <frameset cols="200,*" frameborder="0" border="0" framespacing="0">
    <frame name="menu" id="menu_frame" src="menu_1.html" marginheight="0"
    marginwidth="0" scrolling="auto" noresize>
    <frame name="content" src="content.html" marginheight="0"
    marginwidth="0" scrolling="auto" noresize>
  </frameset>
</frameset>
```

To test a frame with Selenium, we need to identify the frame first by ID or name, and then switch the focus on it. The test steps that follow will be executed in the context of selected frame. Use SwitchTo().DefaultContent() to get back to the page (which contains frames).

```
driver.SwitchTo().Frame("topNav"); // name
driver.FindElement(By.LinkText("Menu 2 in top frame")).Click();
```

```
// need to switch to default before another switch
driver.SwitchTo().DefaultContent();
driver.SwitchTo().Frame("menu_frame"); // not working for Chrome, fine for Firefox
driver.FindElement(By.LinkText("Green Page")).Click();   .

driver.SwitchTo().DefaultContent();
driver.SwitchTo().Frame("content");
driver.FindElement(By.LinkText("Back to original page")).Click();
```

This script clicks a link in each of three frames: top, left menu, and content.

Testing iframe

An inline frame, or iframe, is a HTML document embedded inside another HTML document on a web page. Figure 11-2 shows an example of an iframe.

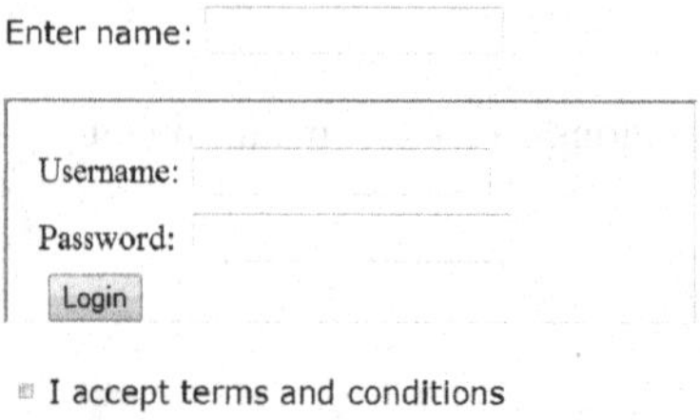

Enter name:

Username:

Password:

Login

▫ I accept terms and conditions

Figure 11-2. *An example of an iframe on a web page*

HTML source

```
<IFRAME frameborder='1' id="Frame1" src="login_iframe.html"
    Style="HEIGHT: 100px; WIDTH: 320px; MARGIN=0" SCROLLING="no" >
</IFRAME>
```

The following test script enters text in the main page, fills the sign-in form in an iframe, and selects the check box on the main page.

```
driver.Navigate().GoToUrl(TestHelper.SiteUrl() + "/iframe.html");
driver.FindElement(By.Name("user")).SendKeys("agileway");

driver.SwitchTo().Frame("Frame1"); // name
driver.FindElement(By.Name("username")).SendKeys("tester");
driver.FindElement(By.Name("password")).SendKeys("TestWise");
driver.FindElement(By.Id("loginBtn")).Click();
Assert.IsTrue(driver.PageSource.Contains("Signed in"));
driver.SwitchTo().DefaultContent();
driver.FindElement(By.Id("accept_terms")).Click();
```

The web page after test execution looks like Figure 11-3.

Enter name: agileway

☑ I accept terms and conditions

Figure 11-3. *A web page after test execution*

Note that the content of the iframe changed, but not the main page.

Test multiple iframes

A web page can contain multiple iframes.

```
driver.SwitchTo().Frame(0);
driver.FindElement(By.Name("username")).SendKeys("agileway");
driver.SwitchTo().DefaultContent();
driver.SwitchTo().Frame(1);
driver.FindElement(By.Id("radio_male")).Click();
```

CHAPTER 12

AJAX

AJAX (an acronym for Asynchronous JavaScript and XML) is widely used in web sites nowadays. Gmail uses AJAX a lot, for example. Let's look at an example first, shown in Figure 12-1. On clicking the Transfer button, an animated loading image indicates that the transfer is in progress.

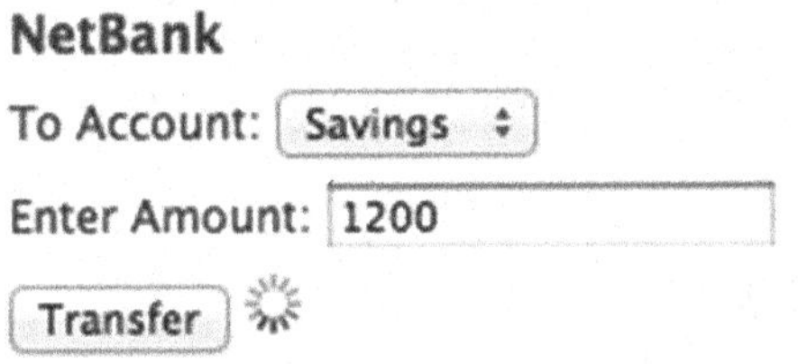

NetBank

To Account: [Savings ▸]

Enter Amount: [1200]

[Transfer] ☼

Figure 12-1. An example of page using AJAX

After the server processes the request, the loading image is gone and a receipt number is displayed, as shown in Figure 12-2.

NetBank

To Account: [Savings ▸]

Enter Amount: [1200]

[Transfer]

Receipt No: 7980
Receipt Date: 02/10/2011

Figure 12-2. Display after the transfer is processed

From a testing perspective, a test step (like clicking the Transfer button) is completed immediately. However, the updates to parts of a web page could happen after an unknown delay, which differs from traditional web requests.

There are two common ways to test AJAX operations: waiting enough time or checking the web page periodically for a maximum given time.

Wait within a time frame

After triggering an AJAX operation (e.g., by clicking a link or button), we can set a timer in our test script to wait for all the asynchronous updates to occur before executing the next step.

```
driver.FindElement(By.XPath("//input[@value='Transfer']")).Click();
System.Threading.Thread.Sleep(10000);
Assert.IsTrue(driver.FindElement(By.TagName("body")).Text.Contains("Receipt No:"));
```

Thread.Sleep(10000) means waiting for 10 seconds after clicking the Transfer button. After that 10 seconds, the test script will check for the Receipt No: text on the page. If the text is present, the test passes; otherwise, the test fails. In other words, if the server finishes the processing and returns the results correctly in 11 seconds, this test execution would be marked as failed.

Explicit waits until time out

Apparently, the waiting for a specified time is not ideal. If the operation finishes earlier, the test execution would still be on halt. Instead of passively waiting, we can write test scripts to define a wait statement for certain conditions to be satisfied until the wait reaches its timeout period. If Selenium can find the element before the defined timeout value, the code execution will continue to the next line of code.

```
driver.FindElement(By.XPath("//input[@value='Transfer']")).Click();
WebDriverWait wait = new WebDriverWait(driver, TimeSpan.FromSeconds(10));
wait.Until(d => d.FindElement(By.Id("receiptNo")) );
```

Implicit waits until time out

An implicit wait is to tell Selenium to poll finding a web element (or elements) for a certain amount of time if they are not immediately available. The default setting is 0. Once set, the implicit wait is set for the life of the WebDriver object instance until its next set.

```
driver.FindElement(By.XPath("//input[@value='Transfer']")).Click();
driver.Manage().Timeouts().ImplicitlyWait(TimeSpan.FromSeconds(10));
Assert.IsTrue(driver.FindElement(By.Id("receiptNo")).Text.Length > 0);
// reset for later steps
driver.Manage().Timeouts().ImplicitlyWait(TimeSpan.FromSeconds(1));
```

Wait AJAX call to complete using JQuery

If the target application uses JQuery for AJAX requests (most do), you can use a JavaScript call to check active AJAX requests: jQuery.active is a variable JQuery uses internally to track the number of simultaneous AJAX requests.

- Drive the control to initiate the AJAX call.

- Wait until the value of jQuery.active is zero.

- Continue the next operation.

The waiting is typically implemented in a reusable function.

```
public void TestWaitUsingJQueryActiveFlag()
{
    driver.Navigate().GoToUrl("http://travel.agileway.net");
    // ...
    driver.FindElement(By.XPath("//input[@value='Pay now']")).Click();
    WaitForAjaxComplete(11);
    Assert.IsTrue(driver.FindElement(By.TagName("body")).Text.
    Contains("Booking number"));
}

public void WaitForAjaxComplete(int maxSeconds)
{
    bool is_ajax_compete = false;
    for (int i = 1; i <= maxSeconds; i++)
    {
        is_ajax_compete = (bool) ((IJavaScriptExecutor)driver).
        ExecuteScript("return window.jQuery != undefined &&
        jQuery.active == 0");
        if (is_ajax_compete)
        {
            return;
        }
        System.Threading.Thread.Sleep(1000);
    }
    throw new Exception("Timed out after " + maxSeconds + " seconds");
}
```

CHAPTER 13

Pop-up

In this chapter, I show you how to handle file upload and popup dialog boxes. Most pop-up dialog boxes, such as Choose File to Upload, are native windows rather than browser windows. This would be a challenge for testing, as Selenium only drives browsers. If one pop-up window is not handled properly, test execution will be halted.

File upload

Figure 13-1 shows a sample file upload page.

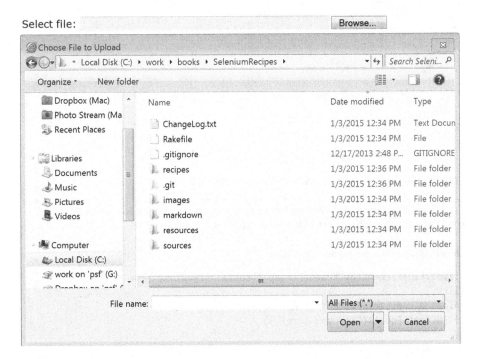

Figure 13-1. Sample file upload page

HTML source

```
<input type="file" name="document[file]" id="files" size="60"/>
```

Test script

```
String filePath = @"c:\work\testdata\users.csv";
driver.FindElement(By.Name("document[file]")).SendKeys(filePath);
```

Hard-coding a file path is not a good practice. It is generally better to include your test data files within your test project, then use relative paths to refer to them, as shown in this example:

```
// ScriptDir() is a helper function returns the  test script directory
String filePath = TestHelper.ScriptDir() + @"\testdata\users.csv";
driver.FindElement(By.Name("document[file]")).SendKeys(filePath);
```

JavaScript pop-ups

JavaScript pop-ups are created using JavaScript, commonly used for confirmation or alerting users. An example is shown in Figure 13-2.

Figure 13-2. *Example of a JavaScript pop-up dialog box*

There are many discussions on handling JavaScript pop-ups in forums and Wikis. I tried several approaches. Here I list two stable ones.

Handle JavaScript pop-ups using Alert API

```
driver.FindElement(By.XPath("//input[contains(@value, 'Buy Now')]")).
Click();
IAlert a = driver.SwitchTo().Alert();
if (a.Text.Equals("Are you sure?"))
{
    a.Accept();
}
```

```
else
{
    a.Dismiss();
}
```

Handle JavaScript pop-ups with JavaScript

```
((IJavaScriptExecutor)driver).ExecuteScript("window.confirm = function() {
return true; }");
((IJavaScriptExecutor)driver).ExecuteScript("window.alert = function() {
return true; }");
((IJavaScriptExecutor)driver).ExecuteScript("window.prompt = function() {
return true; }");
driver.FindElement(By.XPath("//input[contains(@value, 'Buy Now')]")).Click();
```

Different from the previous approach, the pop-up dialog box is not even shown.

Modal style dialog boxes

Flexible JavaScript libraries, such as Bootstrap Modals, replace the default JavaScript alert dialog boxes used in modern web sites. Strictly speaking, a modal dialog box like the one shown in Figure 13-3 is not a pop-up.

Figure 13-3. *A modal dialog box*

Comparing to the raw JavaScript *alert*, writing automated tests against modal pop-ups is easier.

```
driver.FindElement(By.Id("bootbox_popup")).Click();
System.Threading.Thread.Sleep(500);
driver.FindElement(By.XPath("//div[@class='modal-footer']/
button[text()='OK']")).Click();
```

Timeout on a test

When a pop-up window is not handled, it blocks the test execution. This is worse than a test failure when running a number of test cases. For operations that are prone to hold-ups, we can add a TimeoutAttribute with a specified maximum time.

```
[TestMethod]
[Timeout(30 * 1000)] // 30 seconds
public void TestTimeout()
{
  // operations here
}
```

The following is a sample test output when a test case execution times out.

```
Test 'TestTimeout' exceeded execution timeout period.
```

Pop-up handler approach

There are other types of pop-ups, too, such as Basic Authentication and Security warning dialog boxes. How to handle them? The fundamental difficulty behind pop-up dialog box handling is that some of these dialog boxes are native windows, not part of the browser, which means they are beyond the testing library's (i.e., Selenium) control.

Here I introduce a generic approach to handle all sorts of pop-up dialog boxes. Set up a monitoring process (let's call it pop-up handler) waiting for notifications of possible new pop-ups. Once the pop-up handler receives one, it will try to handle the pop-up dialog box with data received using windows automation technologies. It works like this:

```
// ...
NOTIFY_HANDLER_ABOUT_TO_TRIGGER_A_POPUP_OPERATION
PERFORM_OPERATION
// ...
```

BuildWise Agent is a tool for executing automated tests on multiple machines in parallel (see Figure 13-4 and Figure 13-5). It has a free utility named Popup Handler that does just that.

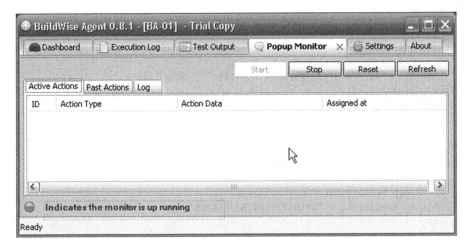

Figure 13-4. *BuildWise Agent Popup Monitor*

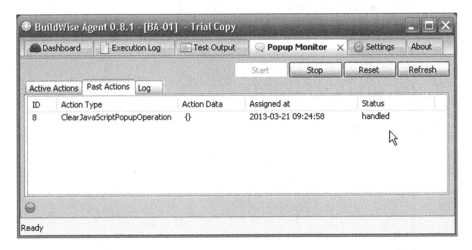

Figure 13-5. *BuildWise Agent Popup Monitor result*

Handle JavaScript dialog with Popup Handler

```
driver.Navigate().GoToUrl("http://testwisely.com/demo/popups");
NotifyPopupHandlerJavaScript("Message from webpage");
driver.FindElement(By.Id("buy_now_btn")).Click();
System.Threading.Thread.Sleep(15000);
driver.FindElement(By.LinkText("NetBank")).Click();
```

The NotifyPopupHandlerJavaScript is a function included in the same project.

```
public static void NotifyPopupHandlerJavaScript(String winTitle)
{
    String handlerPath = "/popup/win_title=" + HttpUtility.
UrlEncode(winTitle);
    GetUrlText(handlerPath);  // notify handler by calling a URL
}

// a helper method to talk to popup handler
public static String GetUrlText(String path)
{
    // Popup Handler URL
    String handlerURL = "http://localhost:4208";
    try
    {
        Uri  website = new Uri(handlerURL + path);
        String urlContent = null;
        using (WebClient client = new WebClient())
        {
            urlContent = client.DownloadString(website);
        }
        return urlContent;
    }
    catch (Exception ex)
    {
        Console.WriteLine("Error: " + ex);
        return "Error";
    }
}
```

Basic or Proxy Authentication dialog box

Figure 13-6 shows an example of a basic authentication dialog box.

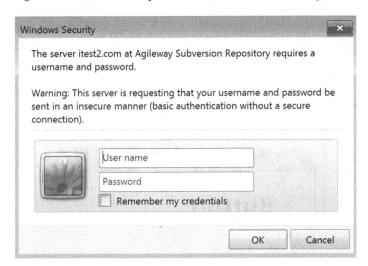

Figure 13-6. *A basic authentication dialog box*

```
String winTitle = "Windows Security";
String username = "tony";
String password = "password";
NotifyPopupHandlerBasicAuth(winTitle, username, password);
driver.Navigate().GoToUrl("http://itest2.com/svn-demo/");
System.Threading.Thread.Sleep(20000);
driver.FindElement(By.LinkText("tony/")).Click();

public static void NotifyPopupHandlerBasicAuth(String winTitle, String
username, String password)
{
    String handlerPath = "/basic_authentication/win_title=" + HttpUtility.
UrlEncode(winTitle) + "&user=" + username + "&password=" + password;
    GetUrlText(handlerPath);
}
```

The same test steps can also be applied to proxy authentication dialog boxes.

Internet Explorer modal dialog box

A modal dialog box, only supported in Internet Explorer, is a dialog box (with the Webpage dialog suffix in the title) that a user has to deal with before interacting with the main web page. It is considered bad practice, and it is rarely found in modern web sites. However, some unfortunate testers might have to deal with modal dialog boxes. Figure 13-7 shows an example page.

Figure 13-7. *Example modal dialog box*

HTML source

```
<a href="javascript:void(0);" onclick="window.showModalDialog('button.
html')">Show Modal Dialog</a>
```

Test script

```
driver.FindElement(By.LinkText("Show Modal Dialog")).Click();

ReadOnlyCollection<String> windowHandles = driver.WindowHandles;
String mainWin = windowHandles[0]; // first one is the main window
String modalWin = windowHandles[windowHandles.Count - 1];

driver.SwitchTo().Window(modalWin);
driver.FindElement(By.Name("user")).SendKeys("in-modal");
driver.SwitchTo().Window(mainWin);
driver.FindElement(By.Name("status")).SendKeys("Done");
```

CHAPTER 14

Debugging Test Scripts

Debugging usually means analyzing and removing bugs in the code. In the context of automated functional testing, debugging is to find out why a test step did not execute as expected and fix it.

Print text for debugging

```
Console.WriteLine("Now on page: " + driver.Title);
String app_no = driver.FindElement(By.Id("app_id")).Text;
Console.WriteLine("Application number is " + app_no);
```

Here is the output from executing that test from the command line:

```
Now on page: Assertion Test Page
Application number is 1234
```

When the test is executed in a continuous integration server, output is normally captured and shown. This can be quite helpful on debugging test execution.

Write page source or element HTML into a file

When the text you want to inspect is large (such as the page source), printing out the text to a console will not be helpful, as there is too much text. A better approach is to write the output to a temporary file and inspect it later

```
// In TestHelper, defines
  public static String TempDir()
  {
    return "C:\\temp";
  }
```

```
using (StreamWriter outfile = new StreamWriter(TestHelper.TempDir() +
@"\login_page.html"))
{
    outfile.Write(driver.PageSource);
}
```

You can also just dump a specific part of a web page.

```
IWebElement the_element = driver.FindElement(By.Id("div_parent"));
String the_element_html = (String)((IJavaScriptExecutor)driver).
    ExecuteScript("return arguments[0].outerHTML;", the_element);

using (StreamWriter outfile = new StreamWriter(TestHelper.TempDir() +
@"\login_parent.xhtml"))
{
    outfile.Write(the_element_html);
}
```

Take a screenshot

Taking a screenshot of the current browser window when an error or failure happens is a good test debugging technique. Selenium supports it in a very easy way.

```
Screenshot ss = ((ITakesScreenshot)driver).GetScreenshot();
ss.SaveAsFile(TestHelper.TempDir() + @"\screenshot.png", System.Drawing.
    Imaging.ImageFormat.Png);
```

This works. However, when it is run the second time, it will return the error "The file already exists". A simple workaround is to write a file with a timestamped file name, as shown here.

```
// save to timestamped file, e.g. Exception-2014-07-14-0422.png
ITakesScreenshot ssdriver = driver as ITakesScreenshot;
Screenshot screenshot = ssdriver.GetScreenshot();
string timestamp = DateTime.Now.ToString("yyyy-MM-dd-hhmm");
screenshot.SaveAsFile(TestHelper.TempDir() + @"\Exception-" + timestamp +
".png", System.Drawing.Imaging.ImageFormat.Png);
```

Leave the browser open after test finishes

Once an error or failure occurs during test execution, a tester's immediate instinct is to check two things: which test statement (using line number for indication) is failed on and what the current web page is like. The first one can be easily found in the testing tools (or command-line output). We need the browser to stay open to see the web page after execution of one test case completes. However, we don't want that when running a group of tests, as it will affect the execution of the following test cases.

Usually we put browser closing statements in @After or @AfterClass fixtures like the following:

```
[ClassCleanup]
public static void AfterAll() {
    driver.Quit();
}
```

Ideally, we would like to keep the browser open after running an individual test case and close the browser when running multiple test script files, within the integrated development environment (IDE). TestWise, an IDE for Selenium Ruby, has this feature. It might be a possible extension you can add to your C# IDE. I can tell you that this feature is quite useful.

Debug test execution using Debugger

Pause, stop execution, and run up to a certain statement are typical debugging features in programming IDEs.

Enable breakpoints

A breakpoint is a stopping or pausing place for debugging purposes. To set a breakpoint, click the left margin next to the line you want to set the breakpoint in, as shown in Figure 14-1.

```
38          select.SelectByText("Cheque");
39          driver.FindElement(By.Id("rcptAmount")).SendKeys("250");
40          driver.FindElement(By.XPath("//input[@value='Transfer']")).Click();
```

Figure 14-1. *Setting a breakpoint*

After it is set, the statement line where the breakpoint occurs is highlighted, as shown in Figure 14-2.

```
38          select.SelectByText("Cheque");
39          driver.FindElement(By.Id("rcptAmount")).SendKeys("250");
40          driver.FindElement(By.XPath("//input[@value='Transfer']")).Click();
```

Figure 14-2. *The line containing the breakpoint highlighted*

You may set more than one breakpoint.

Execute one test case in debugging mode

To start debugging one test case, right-click within the lines of the selected test case and select Debug Tests as shown in Figure 14-3.

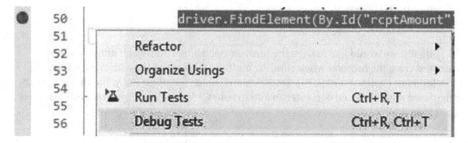

Figure 14-3. Debugging a test case

Test execution starts, although it will be a little slower in debugging mode (see Figure 14-4).

```
50    driver.FindElement(By.Id("rcptAmount")).SendKeys("250");
51    driver.FindElement(By.XPath("//input[@value='Transfer']")).Click();
52    WebDriverWait wait = new WebDriverWait(driver, TimeSpan.FromSeconds(10));  // seconds
```

Figure 14-4. Running a test in debugging mode

Once the test execution is halted, you can do an inspection against the web page.

Step over test execution

To continue test execution, click the Step Over button on the toolbar, as shown in Figure 14-5.

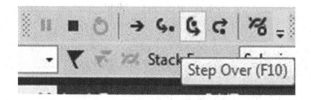

Figure 14-5. Starting test execution

This will execute just the one test statement line. After that, the execution remains in paused mode again.

CHAPTER 15

Test Data

Gathering test data is an important but often neglected activity. With the power of C# programming, testers now have a new ability to prepare test data.

Get date dynamically

```
// assume today is 2014-12-29
String todaysDate = DateTime.Now.ToString("MM/dd/yyyy");
Console.WriteLine("todaysDate = " + todaysDate);
driver.FindElement(By.Name("username")).SendKeys(todaysDate); //=>12/29/2014
```

A more flexible way is to write some helper functions to return common dates.

```
Today("dd/MM/yyyy"); // => 29/12/2014
Tomorrow("AUS");     // => 30/12/2014
Yesterday("ISO");    // => 2014-12-28

public static String GetDate(String format, int dateDiff)
{
    if (format == null)
    {
        format = "MM/dd/yyyy";
    }
    else if (format.Equals("AUS") || format.Equals("UK"))
    {
        format = "dd/MM/yyyy";
    }
    else if (format.Equals("ISO"))
    {
        format = "yyyy-MM-dd";
    }
```

```
    DateTime today = DateTime.Today;
    return today.AddDays(dateDiff).ToString(format);
}

public static String Today(String format)
{
    return GetDate(format, 0);
}

public static String Tomorrow(String format)
{
    return GetDate(format, 1);
}

public static String Yesterday(String format)
{
    return GetDate(format, -1);
}
```

Example use

```
driver.FindElement(By.Id("date")).Text.Equals(Today("MM/dd/yyyy"));
```

Get a random boolean value

A boolean value means either *true* or *false*. Getting a random true or false might not sound that interesting. That was what I thought when I first learned it. Later, I realized that it is actually very powerful, because I can fill the computer program (and test script as well) with nondeterministic data.

```
public static Boolean GetRandomBoolean()
{
    int random_0_or_1 = new Random().Next(0, 2);
    return random_0_or_1 > 0 ? true : false;
}
```

Please note that in C#, when creating a new Random instance new Random() for every random number in quick succession, you are likely to seed them with identical values and have them generate identical random numbers. The following statements will generate the same values (either true or false).

```
GetRandomBoolean();    // true
GetRandomBoolean();    // false
GetRandomBoolean();    // true
```

To solve this, a common practice is to initialize the Random instance at the class level, and always uses it to generate random values.

```
static Random _random;

[ClassInitialize]
public static void BeforeAll(TestContext context)
{
    _random = new Random();
}

// ...
public static Boolean GetRandomBoolean()
{
    int random_0_or_1 = _random.Next(0, 2);
    return random_0_or_1 > 0 ? true : false;
}
```

For example, in a user sign-up form, we could write two cases: one for male and one for female. With random boolean, I could achieve the same with just one test case. If the test case gets run many times, it will cover both scenarios.

```
String randomGender = GetRandomBoolean() ? "male" : "female";
driver.FindElement(By.XPath("//input[@type='radio' and @name='gender' and
@value='" + randomGender + "']")).Click();
```

Generate a number within a range

```
// a number within a range
public static int GetRandomNumber(int min, int max)
{
    return _random.Next(min, max);
}
```

The following test statement will enter a number between 16 and 99. If the test gets run hundreds of times, not a problem at all for an automated test, it will cover driver's input for all permitted ages.

```
// return a number between 16 and 99
driver.FindElement(By.Name("drivers_age")).SendKeys("" + GetRandomNumber(16, 99));
```

Get a random character

```
public static char GetRandomChar()
{
    int num = _random.Next(0, 26); // Zero to 25
    char let = (char)('A' + num);
    return let;
}
```

Get a random string at fixed length

```
public static String GetRandomString(int length)
{
    StringBuilder sb = new StringBuilder();
    for (int i = 0; i < length; i++)
    {
        sb.Append(GetRandomChar());
    }
    return sb.ToString();
}
```

```
[TestMethod]
public void GestRandomStringForTextField() throws Exception {
    // ...
    driver.FindElement(By.Name("password")).SendKeys(GetRandomString(8));
}
```

By creating some utility functions (you can find in them the source project), we can get quite readable test scripts as follows:

```
GetRandomString(7); // example: "dolorem"
GetRandomwords(5);   // example: "sit dolorem consequatur accusantium aut"
GetRandomSentences(3);
GetParagraphs(2);
```

Get a random string in a collection

```
public static String GetRandomStringIn(String[] array)
{
    return array[GetRandomNumber(0, array.Length - 1)];
}
```

```
//...
```

```
[TestMethod]
public void TestRandomStringInCollection()
{
    // SiteUrl is a helper method returns the test server URL
    driver.Navigate().GoToUrl(TestHelper.SiteUrl() + "/text_field.html");

    // one of these strings
    String[] allowableStrings = new String[] { "Yes", "No", "Maybe" };
        driver.FindElement(By.Name("username")).SendKeys(GetRandomStringIn
        (allowableStrings));
}
```

I frequently use this in my test scripts.

Generate a test file at fixed sizes

When testing file uploads, testers often try test files in different sizes. The following Ruby statement generates a test file in precise size on the fly.

```
String outputFilePath = TestHelper.TempDir() + @"\2MB.txt";
File.WriteAllBytes( outputFilePath,  new byte[1024 * 1024 * 2]);
```

Retrieve data from database

The ultimate way to obtain accurate test data is to get it from a database. For many projects, this might not be possible. When it is possible, this provides the ultimate flexibility in terms of getting test data. Figure 15-1 shows a snapshot of a sample database.

rowid	login	name	age
1	zhimin	Zhimin Zhan	36
2	mark	Mark Herb	76
3	eileen	Eileen Jones	10

Figure 15-1. *data in users table*

The following test script example is to enter the oldest (by age) user's login into the text field on a web page. To get this oldest user in the system, I use SQL to query a SQLite3 database directly (it will be different for yours, but the concept is the same) using System.Data.SQLite.

First of all, we need to install the NuGet package of SQLite.

```
PM> Install-Package System.Data.SQLite
```

Then we have the script:

```
String oldestUserLogin = null;
SQLiteConnection connection = null;

try
{
    // database connection string
String dbFile = TestHelper.ScriptDir() + @"\testdata\sample.db";
    connection = new SQLiteConnection("Data Source=" + dbFile + ";Version=3");

    // connect to the database
    connection.Open();

    // execute SQL query
    String sql = "select login from users order by age desc";
    SQLiteCommand command = new SQLiteCommand(sql, connection);

    // process the result set to get the data we want
    SQLiteDataReader reader = command.ExecuteReader();
    while (reader.Read())
    {   // read the result set
        oldestUserLogin = (String) reader["login"];
        break;
    }
}
catch (Exception e)
{
    // probably means no database file is found
    Console.WriteLine(e.Message);
}
finally
{
    try
    {
        if (connection != null)
        {
            connection.Close();
        }
    }
    catch (Exception e)
    { // connection close failed.
        Console.WriteLine(e);
    }
}

Console.WriteLine(" => "+ oldestUserLogin );
driver.FindElement(By.Id("user")).SendKeys(oldestUserLogin);
```

CHAPTER 16

Browser Profile

Selenium WebDriver can start browser instances with various profile preferences, which can be quite useful. Obviously, some preference settings are browser specific, so you should take some time to explore. In this chapter, I cover some common usage.

Get browser type and version

Detecting browser type and version is useful to write custom test scripts for different browsers.

```
driver = new FirefoxDriver();
ICapabilities caps = ((RemoteWebDriver)driver).Capabilities;
String browserName = caps.BrowserName;
String browserVersion = caps.Version;
Console.WriteLine("browserName = " + browserName);        // firefox
Console.WriteLine("browserVersion = " + browserVersion);// 40.0.3
driver.Quit();

driver = new ChromeDriver();
caps = ((RemoteWebDriver)driver).Capabilities;
Platform browserPlatform = caps.Platform;
Console.WriteLine("browserName = " + caps.BrowserName); // chrome
Console.WriteLine("browserVersion = " + caps.Version);   // 46.0.2490.86
Console.WriteLine("browserPlatform = " + browserPlatform.ToString());// Any
driver.Quit();

driver = new InternetExplorerDriver();
caps = ((RemoteWebDriver)driver).Capabilities;
Console.WriteLine("browserName = " + caps.BrowserName); // internet explorer
Console.WriteLine("browserVersion = " + caps.Version);   // 11
driver.Quit();

driver = new EdgeDriver();
caps = ((RemoteWebDriver)driver).Capabilities;
Console.WriteLine("browserName = " + caps.BrowserName); // MicrosoftEdge
Console.WriteLine("browserVersion = " + caps.Version);   // ""
driver.Quit();
```

Set HTTP proxy for browser

Here is an example of how to set the HTTP proxy server for the Firefox browser.

```
FirefoxProfile firefoxProfile = new FirefoxProfile();
firefoxProfile.SetPreference("network.proxy.type", 1);
// See http://kb.mozillazine.org/Network.proxy.type

firefoxProfile.SetPreference("network.proxy.http", "myproxy.com");
firefoxProfile.SetPreference("network.proxy.http_port", 3128);
driver = new FirefoxDriver(firefoxProfile);
driver.Navigate().GoToUrl("http://itest2.com/svn-demo/");
```

Verify file download in Chrome

To efficiently verify that a file is downloaded, we would like to save the file to a specific folder and avoid the Save File dialog box.

```
String myDownloadFolder = @"c:\temp\";
var options = new ChromeOptions();
options.AddUserProfilePreference("download.default_directory", myDownloadFolder);
driver = new ChromeDriver(options);
driver.Navigate().GoToUrl("http://zhimin.com/books/pwta");
driver.FindElement(By.LinkText("Download")).Click();
System.Threading.Thread.Sleep(10000); // wait 10 seconds for downloading

// Assertion using NUnit.Framework
Assert.IsTrue(File.Exists(@"c:\temp\practical-web-test-automation-sample.pdf")) ;
```

This is the new way (from v2.37) to pass preferences to Chrome. More Chrome preferences can be found at http://src.chromium.org/svn/trunk/src/chrome/common/pref_names.cc.

Verify file download in Firefox

```
String myDownloadFolder = @"c:\temp\";
FirefoxProfile fp = new FirefoxProfile();
fp.SetPreference("browser.download.folderList", 2);
fp.SetPreference("browser.download.dir", myDownloadFolder);
fp.SetPreference("browser.helperApps.neverAsk.saveToDisk", "application/pdf");
// disable Firefox's built-in PDF viewer
fp.SetPreference("pdfjs.disabled", true);
```

```
driver = new FirefoxDriver(fp);
driver.Navigate().GoToUrl("http://zhimin.com/books/selenium-recipes");
driver.FindElement(By.LinkText("Download")).Click();
System.Threading.Thread.Sleep(10000); // wait 10 seconds for download

Assert.IsTrue(File.Exists(@"c:\temp\selenium-recipes-in-ruby-sample.pdf"));
```

Bypass basic authentication by embedding username and password in URL

Authentication dialog boxes, like the one shown in Figure16-1, can be troublesome for automated testing.

Figure 16-1. *A HTTP basic authentication dialog box*

A very simple way to get past Basic or NTLM authentication dialog boxes is to prefix username and password in the URL.

```
driver = new FirefoxDriver();
driver.Navigate().GoToUrl("http://tony:password@itest2.com/svn-demo/");
// got in, click a link
driver.FindElement(By.LinkText("tony/")).Click();
System.Threading.Thread.Sleep(1000);
driver.Quit();
```

Bypass basic authentication with Firefox AutoAuth plug-in

There is another complex but quite useful approach to bypassing basic authentication: Use a browser extension. Take Firefox, for example: "Auto Login" submits HTTP authentication dialog boxes remembered passwords.

By default, Selenium starts Firefox with an empty profile, which means there are no remembered passwords and extensions. We can instruct Selenium to start Firefox with an existing profile.

1. Start Firefox with a dedicated profile.

    Run this command (from command line in Windows):

    ```
    "C:\Program Files (x86)\Mozilla Firefox\firefox.exe" -p
    ```

2. Create a profile (I name it **testing** in Figure16-2) and start Firefox with this profile.

Figure 16-2. *Creatig a profile*

3. Install the AutoAuth plug-in.

    For a simple method, drag the file `autoauth-2.1-fx+fn.xpi` (included with the test project) to the Firefox window. The result is shown in Figure16-3.

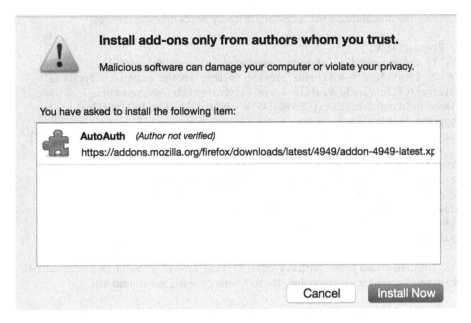

Figure 16-3. Installing the AutoAuth plug-in

4. Visiting the web site requires authentication. Manually type the username and password. Click Remember password, shown Figure16-4.

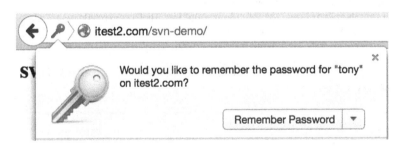

Figure 16-4. Storing a username and password

Now the preparation work is done (and it only needs to be done once).

```
// Prerequisite:
// 1. the password is already remembered in 'testing' profile.
// 2. Identified the firefox profile folder, in the example, '8yggbtss'
FirefoxProfile firefoxProfile = new FirefoxProfile(Environment.
ExpandEnvironmentVariables("%APPDATA%") + @"\Mozilla\Firefox\Profiles\
8yggbtss.testing");
firefoxProfile.AddExtension(TestHelper.ScriptDir() + @"\autoauth-2.1-fx+fn.xpi");

driver = new FirefoxDriver(firefoxProfile);
driver.Navigate().GoToUrl("http://itest2.com/svn-demo/");
// got in, click a link
driver.FindElement(By.LinkText("tony/")).Click();
System.Threading.Thread.Sleep(1000);
driver.Quit();
```

The hard-coded profile path 8yggbtss.testing is not ideal, as the test script will fail when running on another machine. The following code will get around that.

```
// Firefox Profile folder has a random string in the front of name, eg.
"8yggbtss.testing"
// This method returns the file path for a given profile name
public static String GetFirefoxProfileFolderByName(String name)
{
    string pathToCurrentUserProfiles = Environment.ExpandEnvironmentVariables
    ("%APPDATA%") + @"\Mozilla\Firefox\Profiles"; // Path to profile
    string[] pathsToProfiles = Directory.GetDirectories
    (pathToCurrentUserProfiles, "*.*", SearchOption.TopDirectoryOnly);
    foreach (var folder in pathsToProfiles)
    {
        if (folder.EndsWith(name))
        {
            return folder;
        }
    }
    return null;
}

// in your test
).
FirefoxProfile firefoxProfile = new FirefoxProfile
(GetFirefoxProfileFolderByName("testing"));
```

Manage cookies

```
driver.Navigate().GoToUrl("http://travel.agileway.net");
driver.Manage().Cookies.AddCookie(new Cookie("foo", "bar"));
var allCookies = driver.Manage().Cookies.AllCookies;
Cookie retrieved = driver.Manage().Cookies.GetCookieNamed("foo");
Assert.AreEqual("bar", retrieved.Value);
```

Headless browser testing with PhantomJS

A headless browser is a web browser without a graphical user interface. The main benefit of headless browser testing is performance. PhantomJS is a headless browser that is built on top of WebKit, the engine behind both Safari and Chrome. First of all, you need to download phantomjs.exe and put it the PATH, just like chromedriver. In actual test scripts in Selenium WebDriver, we treat PhantomJS just like another browser.

```
using OpenQA.Selenium.PhantomJS;
//...

IWebDriver driver = new PhantomJSDriver();
driver.Navigate().GoToUrl("http://travel.agileway.net");
driver.FindElement(By.Id("username")).SendKeys("agileway");
//...
driver.Quit();
```

If your target application is relatively stable and not using JavaScript heavily, and you want to gain faster test execution time, PhantomJS is a viable option.

Frankly, I am not big fan of headless browser testing for these reasons:

- It is not a real browser.

- I need to inspect the web page when a test fails, and I cannot do that with PhantomJS. In test automation, as we know, we perform this function all the time.

- To achieve faster execution time, I prefer distributing tests to multiple build agents to run them in parallel as a part of a continuous testing process. That way, I get not only much faster execution time (by throwing in more machines), but I also get useful features such as quick feedback, the ability to rerun failed tests on another build agent, dynamic execution ordering by priority, and more, all in real browsers.

Test responsive web sites

Modern web sites embrace responsive design to fit in different screen resolutions on various devices, such as iPads and smartphones. Bootstrap is a very popular responsive framework. How you can verify your web site's responsiveness is a big question, and the answer depends on what you want to test. A quick answer is to use WebDriver's driver.Manage().Window.Size to set your browser to a target resolution, and then execute tests.

The following example verifies a text box's width changes when switching from a desktop computer to an iPad, basically, whether responsive design is enabled or not.

```
driver.Manage().Window.Size = new System.Drawing.Size(1024, 768); //Desktop
driver.Url = "https://support.agileway.net";
int widthDesktop = driver.FindElement(By.Name("email")).Size.Width;
driver.Manage().Window.Size = new System.Drawing.Size(768, 1024); // iPad
int widthIPad = driver.FindElement(By.Name("email")).Size.Width;
Console.WriteLine(widthIPad);
Assert.IsTrue(widthDesktop < widthIPad); // 358 vs 960
```

■ ■ ■

CHAPTER 17

Advanced User Interactions

The Actions in Selenium WebDriver provide a way to set up and perform complex user interactions. Specifically, you can group a series of keyboard and mouse operations and send them to the browser.

Mouse interactions

- Click()
- ClickAndHold()
- ContextClick()
- DoubleClick()
- DragAndDrop()
- DragAndDropToOffset()
- MoveByOffset()
- MoveToElement()
- Release()

Keyboard interactions

- KeyDown()
- KeyUp()
- SendKeys()

The Usage

```
using OpenQA.Selenium.Interactions;
// ...
new Actions(driver). + one or more above operations + .Perform();
```

Check out the Actions API (http://selenium.googlecode.com/git/docs/api/dotnet/html/Methods_T_OpenQA_Selenium_Interactions_Actions.htm) for more.

Double-click a control

```
IWebElement elem = driver.FindElement(By.Id("pass"));
Actions builder = new Actions(driver);
builder.DoubleClick(elem).Perform();
```

Move mouse to a control: Mouse over

```
IWebElement elem = driver.FindElement(By.Id("email"));
Actions builder = new Actions(driver);
builder.MoveToElement(elem).Perform();
```

Click and hold: Select multiple items

The following test script clicks and holds to select three controls in a grid, as shown in Figure 17-1.

```
driver.Navigate().GoToUrl("http://jqueryui.com/selectable");
driver.FindElement(By.LinkText("Display as grid")).Click();
System.Threading.Thread.Sleep(500);
driver.SwitchTo().Frame(0);
ReadOnlyCollection<IWebElement> listItems = driver.FindElements(By.XPath
("//ol[@id='selectable']/li"));
Actions builder = new Actions(driver);
builder.ClickAndHold(listItems[1])
      .ClickAndHold(listItems[3])
      .Click()
      .Perform();
driver.SwitchTo().DefaultContent();
```

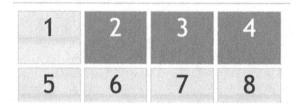

Figure 17-1. *Three controls selected in a grid*

Context click: Right-click a control

```
driver.Navigate().GoToUrl(TestHelper.SiteUrl() + "/text_field.html");
System.Threading.Thread.Sleep(500);
IWebElement elem = driver.FindElement(By.Id("pass"));

ICapabilities caps = ((RemoteWebDriver)driver).Capabilities;
if (caps.BrowserName == "firefox")
{
    Actions builder = new Actions(driver);
    builder.ContextClick(elem)
            .SendKeys(Keys.Down)
            .SendKeys(Keys.Down)
            .SendKeys(Keys.Down)
            .SendKeys(Keys.Down)
            .SendKeys(Keys.Return)
            .Perform();
}
else
{
    // ...
}
```

Drag-and-drop

Drag-and-drop is increasingly more common in new web sites. Testing this feature can be largely achieved in Selenium. I used the word *largely* to mean achieving the same outcome, but not the mouse dragging' part. For the example page shown in Figure 17-2, the following test script will *drop* Item 1 to Trash.

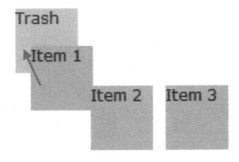

Figure 17-2. Using a drag-and-drop function

```
//this works OK on Chrome, error on Firefox, IE no effect
driver.Navigate().GoToUrl(TestHelper.SiteUrl() + "/drag_n_drop.html"));
IWebElement dragFrom = driver.FindElement(By.Id("item_1"));
IWebElement target = driver.FindElement(By.Id("trash"));

Actions builder = new Actions(driver);
IAction dragAndDrop = builder.ClickAndHold(dragFrom)
        .MoveToElement(target)
        .Release(target).Build();

dragAndDrop.Perform();
```

Figure 17-3 is a screenshot after the test execution.

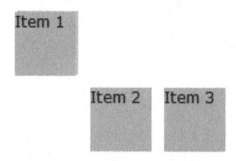

Figure 17-3. *The result of the drag-and-drop execution*

Drag slider

Slider (a part of the JQuery UI library), shown in Figure 17-4, provides users with a very intuitive way to adjust values (typically in settings).

Slider

Figure 17-4. *Using a slider to adjust settings*

The following test simulates dragging the slider to the right.

```
// this does not work on Firefox, yet
Assert.AreEqual("15%", driver.FindElement(By.Id("pass_rate")).Text);
IWebElement elem = driver.FindElement(By.Id("pass-rate-slider"));

Actions move = new Actions(driver);
move.DragAndDropToOffset(elem, 30, 0).Perform();
Assert.AreNotEqual("15%", driver.FindElement(By.Id("pass_rate")).Text);
```

More information about DragAndDropToOffset() can be found in the Selenium Actions .NET API.

Figure 17-5 is a screenshot after the test execution.

Slider

Figure 17-5. *How the slider appears after test execution*

Note that the value (percentage) after executing the preceding test is always 50% (I saw 49% now and then).

Send key sequences: Select All and Delete

```
driver.Navigate().GoToUrl(TestHelper.SiteUrl() + "/text_field.html");
driver.FindElement(By.Id("comments")).SendKeys("Multiple Line\r\n Text");
IWebElement elem = driver.FindElement(By.Id("comments"));

Actions builder = new Actions(driver);
builder.Click(elem)
        .KeyDown(Keys.Control)
        .SendKeys("a")
        .KeyUp(Keys.Control)
        .Perform();
// this different from click element, the key is send to browser directly
builder = new Actions(driver);
builder.SendKeys(Keys.Backspace).Perform();
```

Note that the last test statement is different from Element.SendKeys(). The keystrokes triggered by Actions.SendKeys() are sent to the active browser window, not a specific element.

■ ■ ■

HTML5 and JavaScript

Web technologies are evolving. HTML5 includes many new features for more dynamic web applications and interfaces. Furthermore, with widespread use of JavaScript (thanks to popular JavaScript libraries such as JQuery), web sites nowadays are much more dynamic. In this chapter, I show some Selenium examples to test HTML5 elements and interactive operations.

Please note that some tests only work on certain browsers (Chrome is your best bet), as some HTML5 features are not yet fully supported in some browsers.

HTML5 email type field

Let's start with a simple one. An email type field, like the one shown in Figure 18-1, is used for input fields that should contain an e-mail address. From the testing point of view, we treat it exactly the same as a normal text field.

Email field

Figure 18-1. *An example email type field*

HTML Source

```
<input id="email" name="email" type="email" style="height:30px; width: 280px;">
```

Test Script

```
driver.FindElement(By.Id("email")).SendKeys("test@wisely.com");
```

HTML5 time field

The HTML5 time field is much more complex, as you can see from Figure 18-2.

Time

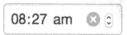

Figure 18-2. *An example of a time field*

HTML Source

```
<input id="start_time_1" name="start_time" type="time" style="height:30px;
width: 120px;">
```

The next test scripts do the following:

1.   Make sure the focus is not on this time field control.

2.   Click and focus the time field.

3.   Clear existing time.

4.   Enter a new time.

```
driver.FindElement(By.Id("start_time_1")).SendKeys("12:05AM");

// focus on another ...
driver.FindElement(By.Id("home_link")).SendKeys("");
System.Threading.Thread.Sleep(500);

// now back to change it
driver.FindElement(By.Id("start_time_1")).Click();
// [:delete, :left, :delete, :left, :delete]
driver.FindElement(By.Id("start_time_1")).SendKeys(Keys.Delete);
driver.FindElement(By.Id("start_time_1")).SendKeys(Keys.Left);
driver.FindElement(By.Id("start_time_1")).SendKeys(Keys.Delete);
driver.FindElement(By.Id("start_time_1")).SendKeys(Keys.Left);
driver.FindElement(By.Id("start_time_1")).SendKeys(Keys.Delete);

driver.FindElement(By.Id("start_time_1")).SendKeys("08");
System.Threading.Thread.Sleep(300);
driver.FindElement(By.Id("start_time_1")).SendKeys("27");
System.Threading.Thread.Sleep(300);
driver.FindElement(By.Id("start_time_1")).SendKeys("AM");
```

Invoke 'onclick' JavaScript event

In the example shown in Figure 18-3, when a user clicks the text field control, the tip text (*Max 20 characters*) is shown.

Max 20 characters

Figure 18-3. *A example onclick event*

HTML Source

```
<input type="text" name="person_name" onclick="$('#tip').show();"
onchange="change_person_name(this.value);"/>
<span id="tip" style="display:none; margin-left: 20px; color:gray;">Max 20
characters</span>
```

When we use normal SendKeys() in Selenium, it enters the text OK, but the tip text is not displayed.

```
driver.FindElement(By.Name("person_name")).SendKeys("Wise Tester");
```

We can simply call Click to achieve it.

```
driver.FindElement(By.Name("person_name")).Clear();
driver.FindElement(By.Name("person_name")).SendKeys("Wise Tester");

driver.FindElement(By.Name("person_name")).Click();
driver.FindElement(By.Id("tip")).Text.Equals("Max 20 characters");
```

Invoke JavaScript events such as onchange

A generic way to invoke OnXXXX events is to execute JavaScript. The following is an example to invoke an OnChange event on a text box.

```
driver.FindElement(By.Id("person_name_textbox")).Clear();
driver.FindElement(By.Id("person_name_textbox")).SendKeys("Wise Tester too");
((IJavaScriptExecutor) driver).ExecuteScript("$('#person_name_textbox').
trigger('change')");
Assert.IsTrue(driver.FindElement(By.Id("person_name_label")).Text.
Equals("Wise Tester too"));
```

Scroll to the bottom of a page

Call the JavaScript API.

```
String js = "window.scrollTo(0, document.body.scrollHeight);";
((IJavaScriptExecutor)driver).ExecuteScript(js);
```

Alternately, you can send the keyboard command Ctrl+End.

```
driver.FindElement(By.TagName("body")).SendKeys(Keys.Control + Keys.End);
```

Chosen: Standard select

Chosen is a popular JQuery plug-in that makes long select lists more user-friendly. It turns the standard HTML select list box into this something that looks like Figure 18-4.

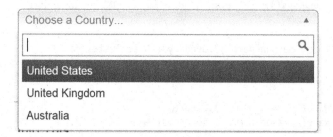

Figure 18-4. *Using the Chosen plug-in*

HTML Source

```
<select id="chosen_single" class="chosen-select"  data-placeholder="Choose a
Country..." style="width:350px;">
  <option value=""></option>
  <option value="United States">United States</option>
  <option value="United Kingdom">United Kingdom</option>
  <option value="Australia">Australia</option>
</select>
```

The HTML source does not seem much different from the standard select list except for the addition of the class chosen-select. By using the class as the identification, the JavaScript included on the page generates the following HTML fragment (beneath the select element).

106

Generated HTML Source

```
<div class="chosen-container chosen-container-single chosen-container-
active" style="width: 350px;" title="" id="chosen_single_chosen">
  <a class="chosen-single chosen-default" tabindex="-1"><span>Choose a
Country...</span><div><b></b></div></a>
  <div class="chosen-drop">
    <div class="chosen-search">
      <input type="text" autocomplete="off" tabindex="2">
    </div>
    <ul class="chosen-results">
      <li class="active-result" style="" data-option-array-index="1">United
      States</li>
      <li class="active-result result-selected" style="" data-option-array-
      index="2">United Kingdom</li>
      <li class="active-result" style="" data-option-array-index="3">Australia</li>
    </ul>
  </div>
</div>
```

Note that this dynamically generated HTML fragment is not viewable using View Page Source. You need to enable the inspection tool (usually by right-clicking the page, then choosing Inspect Element) to see it.

Before we test it, we need to understand how we use it.

- Click Choose a Country.

- Select an option.

There is no difference from the standard select list. That's correct: We need to understand how Chosen emulates the standard select list first. In Chosen, clicking Choose a Country is actually clicking a hyperlink with class "chosen-single" under the div with ID "chosen_single_chosen" (the ID is whatever is set in the select element, followed by '_chosen'); selecting an option is clicking an list item (tag: li) with class 'active-result'. With that knowledge, plus XPath in Selenium, we can drive a Chosen standard select box with these test scripts.

```
System.Threading.Thread.Sleep(2000);  // wait enough time to load JS
driver.FindElement(By.XPath("//div[@id='chosen_single_chosen']//a[contains
(@class,'chosen-single')]")).Click();
ReadOnlyCollection<IWebElement> available_items = driver.FindElements
(By.XPath("//div[@id='chosen_single_chosen']//div[@class='chosen-drop']
//li[contains(@class,'active-result')]"));
foreach (IWebElement item in available_items)
{
    if (item.Text.Equals("Australia")) {
        item.Click();
        break;
    }
}
```

```
System.Threading.Thread.Sleep(1000);

driver.FindElement(By.XPath("//div[@id='chosen_single_chosen']//a[contains
(@class,'chosen-single')]")).Click();
available_items = driver.FindElements(By.XPath("//div[@id='chosen_
single_chosen']//div[@class='chosen-drop']//li[contains(@class,'active-
result')]"));
foreach (IWebElement item in available_items)
{
    if (item.Text.Equals("United States")) {
        item.Click();
        break;
    }
}
```

A neat feature of Chosen is allowing the user to search the option list. To do that in Selenium, follow this script.

```
System.Threading.Thread.Sleep(1000);
driver.FindElement(By.XPath("//div[@id='chosen_single_chosen']//a[contains
(@class,'chosen-single')]")).Click();

IWebElement searchTextField = driver.FindElement(By.XPath
("//div[@id='chosen_single_chosen']//div[@class='chosen-drop']//div[contains
(@class,'chosen-search')]/input"));
searchTextField.SendKeys("United King");
System.Threading.Thread.Sleep(500); // let filtering finishing
// select first selected option
searchTextField.SendKeys(Keys.Enter);
```

Chosen: Multiple select

Chosen also significantly enhances multiple selection, shown in Figure 18-5.

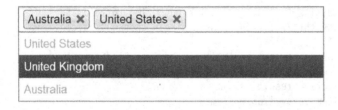

Figure 18-5. *Using Chosen for multiple selection*

HTML Source

```
<select id="chosen_multiple" class="chosen-select" multiple
data-placeholder="Choose a Country..."  style="width:350px;">
    <option value=""></option>
    <option value="United States">United States</option>
    <option value="United Kingdom">United Kingdom</option>
    <option value="Australia">Australia</option>
</select>
```

Again, the only difference in HTML from the standard multiple select list is the class chosen-select.

Generated HTML Source

```
<div class="chosen-container chosen-container-multi chosen-container-active"
style="width: 350px;" title="" id="chosen_multiple_chosen">
  <ul class="chosen-choices">
    <li class="search-choice"><span>Australia</span><a class="search-choice-
    close" data-option-array-index="3"></a></li>
    <li class="search-choice"><span>United States</span><a class="search-
    choice-close" data-option-array-index="1"></a></li>
    <li class="search-field"><input type="text" value="Choose a Country..."
    class="" autocomplete="off" style="width: 25px;" tabindex="4"></li>
  </ul>
  <div class="chosen-drop">
    <ul class="chosen-results">
      <li class="result-selected" style="" data-option-array-
      index="1">United States</li>
      <li class="active-result" style="" data-option-array-index="2">United
      Kingdom</li>
      <li class="result-selected" style="" data-option-array-index="3">Australia</li>
      </ul>
  </div>
</div>
```

Astute readers will find the generated HTML fragment is quite different from the standard (single) select because of the usage. The concept of working out driving the control is the same. I will leave the homework to you, and just show the test scripts here.

```
System.Threading.Thread.Sleep(2000);  // wait enough time to load JS
driver.FindElement(By.XPath("//div[@id='chosen_multiple_chosen']
//li[@class='search-field']/input")).Click();
ReadOnlyCollection<IWebElement> available_items = driver.FindElements
(By.XPath("//div[@id='chosen_multiple_chosen']//div[@class='chosen-drop']
//li[contains(@class,'active-result')]"));
```

109

```
foreach (IWebElement item in available_items) {
    if (item.Text.Equals("Australia")) {
        item.Click();
        break;
    }
}
System.Threading.Thread.Sleep(1000);

// select another
driver.FindElement(By.XPath("//div[@id='chosen_multiple_chosen']
//li[@class='search-field']/input")).Click();
available_items = driver.FindElements(By.XPath("//div[@id='chosen_
multiple_chosen']//div[@class='chosen-drop']//li[contains(@class,'active-
result')]"));
foreach (IWebElement item in available_items) {
    if (item.Text.Equals("United Kingdom")) {
        item.Click();
        break;
    }
}
```

To deselect an option is to click the little x on the right. In fact, the idea is to clear all selections first, then select the desired options.

```
System.Threading.Thread.Sleep(500);
// clear all selections
ReadOnlyCollection<IWebElement> closeButtons = driver.FindElements
(By.XPath("//div[@id='chosen_multiple_chosen']//ul[@class='chosen-choices']/
li[contains(@class,'search-choice')]/a[contains(@class,'search-choice-
close')]"));
    foreach (IWebElement item in closeButtons) {
    item.Click();
}

// then select specific one after clear
driver.FindElement(By.XPath("//div[@id='chosen_multiple_chosen']
//li[@class='search-field']/input")).Click();
available_items = driver.FindElements(By.XPath("//div[@id='chosen_multiple_
chosen']//div[@class='chosen-drop']//li[contains(@class,'active-result')]"));
foreach (IWebElement item in available_items)
{
    if (item.Text.Equals("United States"))
    {
        item.Click();
        break;
    }
}
```

Some might say the test scripts are quite complex. That's good thinking; if many of our test steps are written like this, it will be quite hard to maintain. One common way to address this is to extract them into reusable functions, as shown here.

```
public void ClearChosen(String elemId) {
    System.Threading.Thread.Sleep(500);
    ReadOnlyCollection<IWebElement> closeButtons = driver.FindElements
    (By.XPath("//div[@id='" + elemId + "']//ul[@class='chosen-choices']/
    li[contains(@class,'search-choice')]/a[contains(@class,'search-choice-
    close')]"));
    foreach (IWebElement closeButton in closeButtons)
    {
        closeButton.Click();
    }
}

public void SelectChosenByLabel(String elemId, String label) {
    driver.FindElement(By.XPath("//div[@id='" + elemId + "']
    //li[@class='search-field']/input")).Click();
    ReadOnlyCollection<IWebElement> availableItems = driver.FindElements
    (By.XPath("//div[@id='" + elemId + "']//div[@class='chosen-drop']
    //li[contains(@class,'active-result')]"));
    foreach (IWebElement item in availableItems)
    {
        if (item.Text.Equals(label)) {
            item.Click();
            break;
        }
    }
}

[TestMethod]
public void TestChosenMultipleCallingMethods()
{
    driver.Navigate().GoToUrl(TestHelper.SiteUrl() + "/chosen/index.html"));
    // ... land to the page with a chosen select list
    ClearChosen("chosen_multiple_chosen");
    SelectChosenByLabel("chosen_multiple_chosen", "United States");
    SelectChosenByLabel("chosen_multiple_chosen", "Australia");
}
```

You can find more techniques for writing maintainable tests in my other book, *Practical Web Test Automation.*

AngularJS web pages

AngularJS is a popular client-side JavaScript framework that can be used to extend HTML. Figure 18-6 is a sample web page (simple TODO list) developed in AngularJS.

1 of 3 remaining [<u>archive</u>]

- ☑ ~~learn angular~~
- ☐ build an angular app
- ☑ ~~Learn test automation~~

add new todo here   add

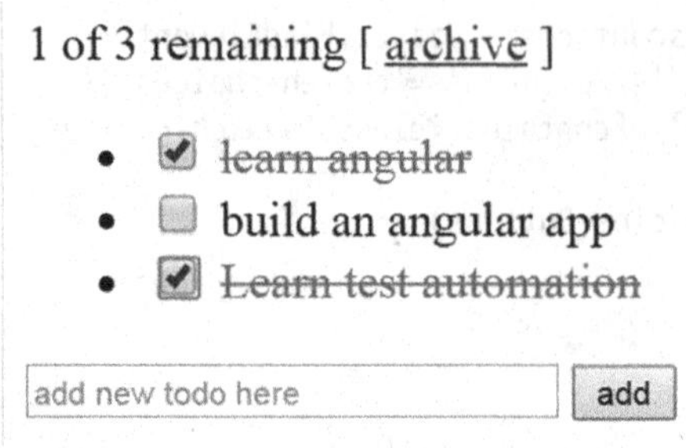

Figure 18-6. *A sample TODO list developed in AngularJS*

HTML Source

The page source (via "View Page Source" in browser) is different from what you saw on the page. It contains some kind of dynamic coding (ng-xxx).

```
<div ng-controller="TodoCtrl">
  <span>{{remaining()}} of {{todos.length}} remaining</span>
  [ <a href="" ng-click="archive()">archive</a> ]
  <ul class="unstyled">
    <li ng-repeat="todo in todos">
      <input type="checkbox" ng-model="todo.done">
      <span class="done-{{todo.done}}">{{todo.text}}</span>
    </li>
  </ul>
  <form ng-submit="addTodo()">
    <input type="text" ng-model="todoText"  size="30"
           placeholder="add new todo here">
    <input class="btn-primary" type="submit" value="add">
  </form>
</div>
```

As a tester, we don't need to worry about AngularJS programming logic in the page source. To view the rendered page source, which matters for testing, inspect the page by right-clicking the page and selecting Inspect Element. That browser view is shown in Figure 18-7.

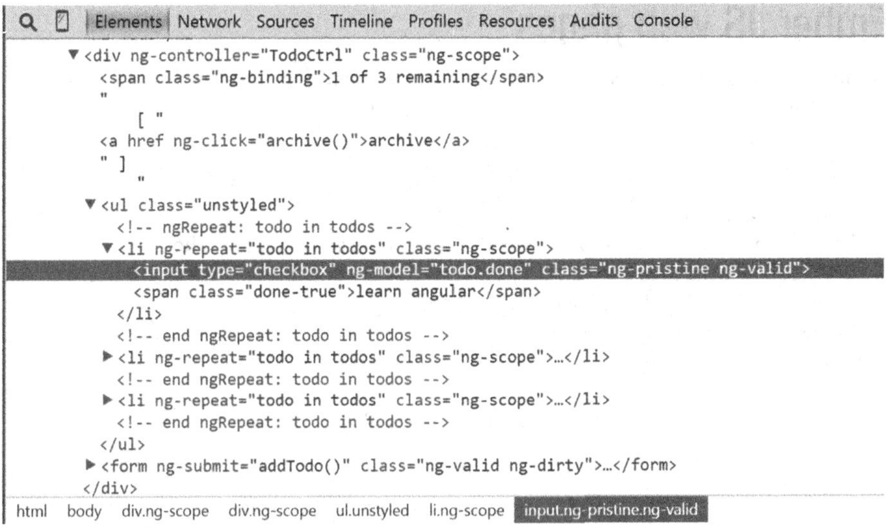

Figure 18-7. Browser inspect view

Astute readers will notice that the `name` attributes are missing in the input elements, replaced with `ng-model` instead. We can use `xpath` to identify the web element.

The following test scripts do the following:

- Add a new todo item in a text field.

- Click the Add button.

- Uncheck the third todo item.

```
Assert.IsTrue(driver.PageSource.Contains("1 of 2 remaining"));
driver.FindElement(By.XPath("//input[@ng-model='todoText']")).
SendKeys("Learn test automation");
driver.FindElement(By.XPath("//input[@type = 'submit' and @value='add']")).
Click();
System.Threading.Thread.Sleep(500);
driver.FindElements(By.XPath("//input[@type = 'checkbox' and @ng-
model='todo.done']"))[2].Click();
System.Threading.Thread.Sleep(1000);
Assert.IsTrue(driver.PageSource.Contains("1 of 3 remaining"));
```

113

Ember JS web pages

Ember JS is another JavaScript web framework. Like Angular JS, the Page Source view (from a browser) of a web page is raw source code, which is not useful for testing.

HTML Source

```
<div class="control-group">
  <label class="control-label" for="longitude">Longitude</label>
  <div class="controls">
    {{view Ember.TextField valueBinding="longitude"}}
  </div>
</div>
```

The browser inspect view is shown in Figure 18-8.

```
▼<div class="control-group">
    ::before
    <label class="control-label" for="longitude">Longitude</label>
  ▼<div class="controls">
      <input id="ember412" class="ember-view ember-text-field" type="text">
    </div>
    ::after
  </div>
```

Figure 18-8. *Browser inspect view*

The ID attribute of an Ember JS generated element (by default) changes. For example, the text field ID in Figure 18-9 is ember412.

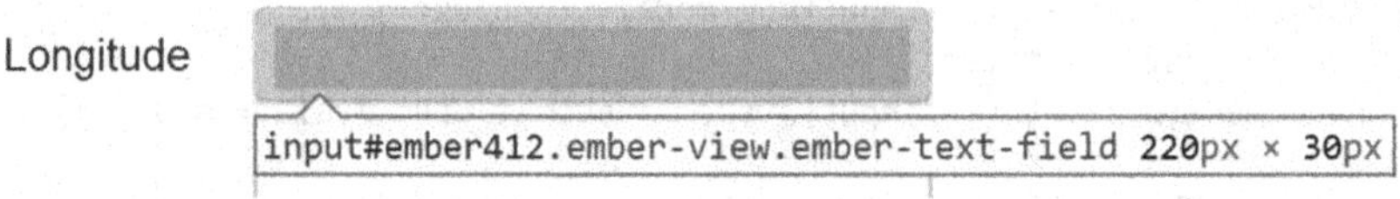

Longitude

```
input#ember412.ember-view.ember-text-field 220px × 30px
```

Figure 18-9. *The initial ID attribute*

When you refresh the page, the ID changes to a different value, as shown in Figure 18-10.

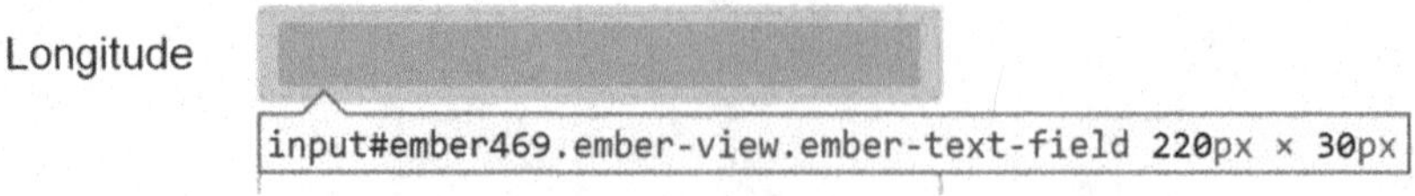

Longitude

```
input#ember469.ember-view.ember-text-field 220px × 30px
```

Figure 18-10. *The new value of the ID*

So we use another way to identify the element.

```
ReadOnlyCollection<IWebElement> emberTextFields = driver.FindElements(By.
XPath("//div[@class='controls']/input[@class='ember-view ember-text-field']"));
emberTextFields[0].SendKeys("-24.0034583945");
emberTextFields[1].SendKeys("146.903459345");
emberTextFields[2].SendKeys("90%");

driver.FindElement(By.XPath("//button[text() ='Update record']")).Click();
```

CHAPTER 19

WYSIWYG Editor

WYSIWYG (an acronym for what you see is what you get) HTML editors are widely used in web applications as embedded text editor. In this chapter, we use Selenium WebDriver to test several popular WYSIWYG HTML editors.

TinyMCE

TinyMCE is a web-based WYSIWYG editor. It claims to be the most used WYSIWYG editor in the world, used by millions. Its interface is shown in Figure 19-1.

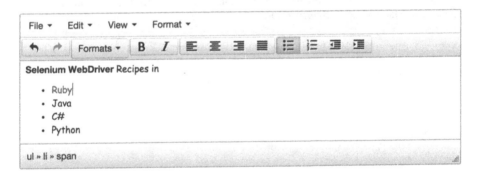

Figure 19-1. The TinyMCE interface

The rich text is rendered inside an inline frame within TinyMCE. To test it, we need to switch to that frame.

```
driver.Navigate().GoToUrl(TestHelper.SiteUrl() + "/tinymce-4.1.9/tinyice_
demo.html"));

IWebElement tinymceFrame = driver.FindElement(By.Id("mce_0_ifr"));
driver.SwitchTo().Frame(tinymceFrame);
IWebElement editorBody = driver.FindElement(By.CssSelector("body"));
((IJavaScriptExecutor)driver).ExecuteScript("arguments[0].innerHTML =
'<h1>Heading</h1>AgileWay'", editorBody);
```

```
System.Threading.Thread.Sleep(500);
editorBody.SendKeys("New content");
System.Threading.Thread.Sleep(500);
editorBody.Clear();

// click TinyMCE editor's 'Numbered List' button
((IJavaScriptExecutor)driver).ExecuteScript("arguments[0].innerHTML =
'<p>one</p><p>two</p>'", editorBody);

// switch out then can drive controls on the main page
driver.SwitchTo().DefaultContent();
IWebElement tinymceNumberListBtn = driver.FindElement(By.CssSelector
(".mce-btn[aria-label='Numbered list'] button"));
tinymceNumberListBtn.Click();

// Insert using JavaScripts
((IJavaScriptExecutor)driver).ExecuteScript("tinyMCE.activeEditor.
insertContent('<p>Brisbane</p>')");
```

CKEditor

CKEditor is another popular WYSIWYG editor. Like TinyMCE, CKEditor uses an inline frame. It interface is shown in Figure 19-2.

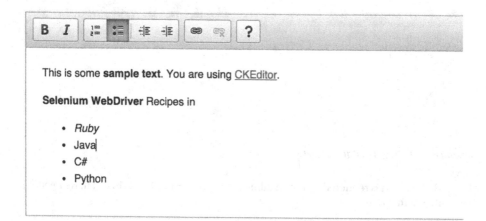

Figure 19-2. The CKEditor interface

```
driver.Navigate().GoToUrl(TestHelper.SiteUrl() + "/ckeditor-4.4.7/samples/
uicolor.html"));
System.Threading.Thread.Sleep(500); // wait to load
IWebElement ckeditorFrame = driver.FindElement(By.ClassName("cke_wysiwyg_
frame"));
```

```
driver.SwitchTo().Frame(ckeditorFrame);
IWebElement editorBody = driver.FindElement(By.TagName("body"));
editorBody.SendKeys("Selenium Recipes\n by Zhimin Zhan");
System.Threading.Thread.Sleep(500);
editorBody.SendKeys("New content");
System.Threading.Thread.Sleep(500);
editorBody.Clear();

// Clear content Another Method Using ActionBuilder to clear()
Actions builder = new Actions(driver);
builder.Click(editorBody)
        .KeyDown(Keys.Control)
        .SendKeys("a")
        .KeyUp(Keys.Control)
        .Perform();
builder.SendKeys(Keys.Backspace)
        .Perform();

// switch out then can drive controls on the main page
driver.SwitchTo().DefaultContent();
// click the numberd list button
driver.FindElement(By.ClassName("cke_button__numberedlist")).Click();
```

SummerNote

SummerNote is a Bootstrap-based lightweight WYSIWYG editor. Unlike TinyMCE or CKEditor, it does not use frames. Its interface is shown in Figure 19-3.

Figure 19-3. *The SummerNote interface*

```
driver.Navigate().GoToUrl(TestHelper.SiteUrl() + "/summernote-0.6.3/
demo.html"));
System.Threading.Thread.Sleep(500);
driver.FindElement(By.XPath("//div[@class='note-editor']/div[@class=
'note-editable']")).SendKeys("Text");
```

119

```
// click a format button: unordered list
driver.FindElement(By.XPath("//button[@data-event='insertUnorderedList']")).
Click();
// switch to code view
driver.FindElement(By.XPath("//button[@data-event='codeview']")).Click();
// insert code (unformatted)
driver.FindElement(By.XPath("//textarea[@class='note-codable']")).
SendKeys("\n<p>HTML</p>");
```

CodeMirror

CodeMirror is a versatile text editor implemented in JavaScript. CodeMirror is not a WYSIWYG editor, but it is often used with one for editing raw HTML source for the rich text content. Its interface is shown in Figure 19-4.

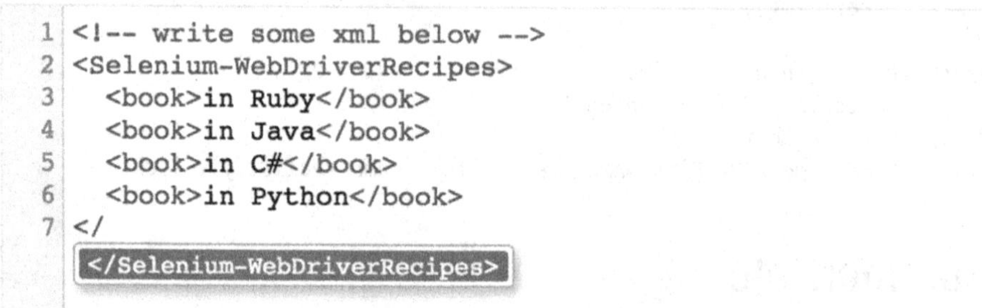

```
1  <!-- write some xml below -->
2  <Selenium-WebDriverRecipes>
3    <book>in Ruby</book>
4    <book>in Java</book>
5    <book>in C#</book>
6    <book>in Python</book>
7  </
   </Selenium-WebDriverRecipes>
```

Figure 19-4. *The CodeMirror interface*

```
driver.Navigate().GoToUrl(TestHelper.SiteUrl() + "/codemirror-5.1/demo/
xmlcomplete.html"));
System.Threading.Thread.Sleep(500);
IWebElement elem = driver.FindElement(By.ClassName("CodeMirror-scroll"));
elem.Click();
System.Threading.Thread.Sleep(500);
// elem.SendKeys does not work
Actions builder = new Actions(driver);
builder.SendKeys("<h3>Heading 3</h3><p>TestWise is Selenium IDE</p>")
       .Perform();
```

CHAPTER 20

Leverage Programming

The reason that Selenium WebDriver quickly overtakes other commercial testing tools (typically promoting record-and-playback), in my opinion, is embracing programming, which offers the flexibility needed for maintainable automated test scripts.

In this chapter, I show some examples that use some programming practices to help our testing needs.

Throw exceptions to fail test

Although Visual Studio Unit Testing Framework or NUnit framework provides most of the assertions needed, throwing exceptions can be useful too, as shown below.

```
string osPlatform = System.Environment.OSVersion.Platform.ToString();
System.Console.WriteLine(osPlatform);
if (osPlatform != "Win32NT")
{
  throw new Exception("Unsupported platform: " + osPlatform);
}
```

In test output (when running on Unix):

```
Unsupported platform: Unix
```

An exception means an anomalous or exceptional condition occurred. The code to handle exceptions is called exception handling, an important concept in programming. If an exception is not handled, the program execution will terminate with the exception displayed.

Here is anther more complete example.

```
try {
  driver = new ChromeDriver();
  // ...
} catch (Exception ex) {
    Console.WriteLine("Exception occurred: " + ex + ", " + ex.StackTrace);
} finally {
  driver.Quit();
}
```

The catch block handles the exception. If an exception is handled, the program (in our case, test execution) continues. ex.StackTrace returns the stack trace of the exception that occurred. The finally block is always run (after) no matter if exceptions are thrown (from try) or not.

I often use exceptions in my test scripts for non-assertion purposes, too.

Flag incomplete tests

The problem with TODO comments is that you might forget them.

```
[TestMethod] public void TestFooBar() {
    // TODO
}
```

I like this way better.

```
[TestMethod] public void TestFooBar() {
  throw new Exception("TO BE DONE");
}
```

Stop test execution during debugging a test

Sometimes, you want to use automated tests to get you to a certain page in the application quickly.

```
// test steps ...
throw new Exception("Stop here, I take over from now. delete this later.")
// ...
```

Ignorable test statement error

When a test step cannot be performed correctly, execution terminates and the test is marked as failed. However, failure to run certain test steps sometimes is okay. For example, we want to make sure a test starts with no active user session. If a user is currently signed in, try signing out. If a user has already signed out, signing out will fail, but it is acceptable.

Here is an example to capture an exception from a test statement, and then ignore.

```
try
{
    driver.FindElement(By.Name("notExists")).Click();
}
catch (Exception ex)
{
    Console.WriteLine("Error occurred:  " + ex + ", but it is OK to ignore");
}
// ...
```

Read external file

We can use C#'s built-in file I/O functions to read data, typically test data, from external files. Try to avoid referencing an external file using absolute path like this:

```
String filePath = @"C:\testdata\in.xml";  // bad
String content = File.ReadAllText(filePath);
// ...
```

If the test script is copied to another machine, it might fail. When you have a lot of references to absolute file paths, it is going to be difficult to maintain. A common practice is to retrieve the test data folder from a reusable function so that it only needs to update once.

```
/* in a helper file */
public static String ScriptDir() {
    return @"C:\work\books\SeleniumRecipes-C#\recipes";
}
```

```
/* in test file */
[TestMethod]
public void TestReadExtnernalFile() throws Exception {
    String filePath = TestHelper.ScriptDir() + @"\testdata\in.xml";
    Assert.IsTrue(File.Exists(filePath));
    String content = File.ReadAllText(filePath);
    Console.WriteLine("content = " + content);
}
```

Data-driven tests with Excel

Data-driven testing means a test's input is driven from external sources, quite commonly in Excel or CSV files. For instance, if there is a list of user credentials with different roles and the login process is the same (but with different assertions), you can extract the test data from an Excel spreadsheet and execute it one by one.

A sample spreadsheet (*users.xls*) contains three username-password combinations, as shown in Table 20-1.

Table 20-1. *Username and Password Combinations*

Description	Login	Password	Expected Text
Valid Login	agileway	testwise	Welcome agileway
User name not exists	notexists	smartass	Login is not valid
Password not match	agileway	badpass	Password is not valid

First of all, make sure that you have Microsoft Office installed with the .NET Programmability Support feature is selected.

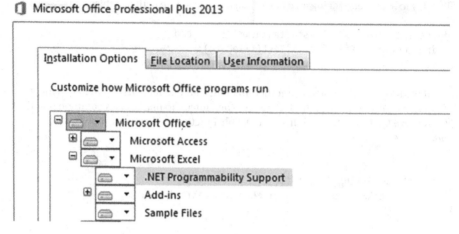

Figure 20-1. *Install Office with .Net support*

To read an Excel spreadsheet in C#, we need to add the `Microsoft.Office.Interop.Excel` assembly to the project. Right click the project references ➤ Add Reference, and select Microsoft Excel 15.0 Object Library under COM as shown in Figure 20-2.

Reference Manager - SeleniumRecipes

	Name	Version
▷ Assemblies		
▷ Projects		
◢ COM	Microsoft DirectX Transforms Core Type Library	1.1
	Microsoft DirectX Transforms Image Transforms...	1.1
Type Libraries	Microsoft Disk Quota 1.0	1.0
Recent	☑ Microsoft Excel 15.0 Object Library	1.8
	Microsoft External Item Picker	1.0

Figure 20-2. *Adding Excel assembly to project*

After adding the assembly successfully, you will see the `Microsoft.Office.Core` and `Microsoft.Office.Interop.Excel` assemblies in the project references as shown in Figure 20-3.

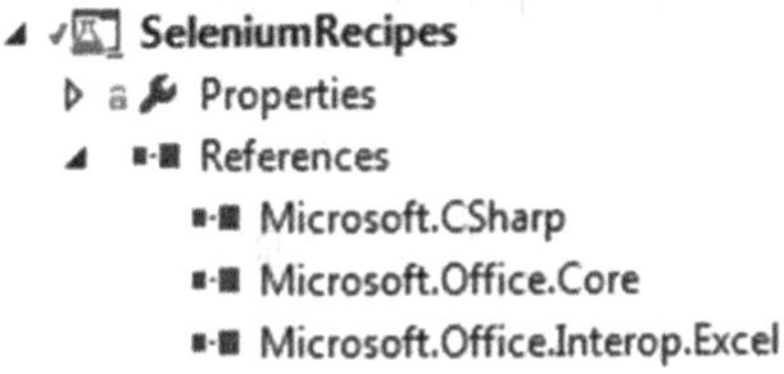

▲ ✓🖳 **SeleniumRecipes**
   ▷ ā 🔑 Properties
   ▲ ■·■ References
        ■·■ Microsoft.CSharp
        ■·■ Microsoft.Office.Core
        ■·■ Microsoft.Office.Interop.Excel

Figure 20-3. *Excel assembly added to the project references*

The following test script below reads the above and uses the login data to drive the browser to perform tests.

```
using Excel = Microsoft.Office.Interop.Excel;

// ...

String filePath = TestHelper.ScriptDir() + @"\testdata\users.xls";
Console.WriteLine("Excel file: " + filePath);
Excel.Application excelApp;
Excel.Workbook excelWorkbook;
Excel.Worksheet sheet;
Excel.Range range;
int rCnt = 0;
int cCnt = 0;

String description = null;
String login = null;
String password = null;
String expectedText = null;

excelApp = new Excel.Application();
// Opening Excel file
excelWorkbook = excelApp.Workbooks.Open(filePath);
sheet = excelWorkbook.Worksheets.get_Item(1);

range = sheet.UsedRange;

// starting from 2, skip the header row
for (rCnt = 2; rCnt <= range.Rows.Count; rCnt++)
{
    Console.WriteLine("1.");

    Excel.Range myIDBinder = (Excel.Range)sheet.get_Range("A" +
    rCnt.ToString(), "A" + rCnt.ToString());
    description = myIDBinder.Value.ToString();
```

```csharp
myIDBinder = (Excel.Range)sheet.get_Range("B" + rCnt.ToString(),
"B" + rCnt.ToString());
login = myIDBinder.Value.ToString();

myIDBinder = (Excel.Range)sheet.get_Range("C" + rCnt.ToString(),
"C" + rCnt.ToString());
password = myIDBinder.Value.ToString();

myIDBinder = (Excel.Range)sheet.get_Range("D" + rCnt.ToString(),
"D" + rCnt.ToString());
expectedText = myIDBinder.Value.ToString();

driver.Navigate().GoToUrl("http://travel.agileway.net");
driver.FindElement(By.Name("username")).SendKeys(login);
driver.FindElement(By.Name("password")).SendKeys(password);
driver.FindElement(By.Name("username")).Submit();
Assert.IsTrue(driver.FindElement(By.TagName("body")).Text.Contains
(expectedText));

try
{
    // if logged in OK, try log out, so next one can continue
    driver.FindElement(By.LinkText("Sign off")).Click();
}
catch (Exception ex)
{
    // ignore
}
}

excelWorkbook.Close(true, null, null);
excelApp.Quit();
```

Data-driven tests with CSV

A comma-separated values (CSV) file stores tabular data in plain text form. CSV files are commonly used for importing into or exporting from applications. Compared to an Excel spreadsheet, a CSV file is a text file that contains only the pure data without formatting.

The following is the CSV version of a data-driven test for the preceding user sign-in example, using the **CSVReader** class (found under the helper folder):

```csharp
// Iterate each row in the CSV file, use data for test scripts
String csvFilePath = TestHelper.ScriptDir() + @"\testdata\users.csv";

IEnumerable<IList<string>> data = CSVReader.FromFile(csvFilePath);
```

```
foreach (IList<string> nextLine in data)
{
    // nextLine[] is an array of values from the line
    String login = nextLine[1];
    String password = nextLine[2];
    String expected_text = nextLine[3];

    if (login.Equals("LOGIN"))
    { // head row
        continue;
    }
    driver.Navigate().GoToUrl("http://travel.agileway.net");
    driver.FindElement(By.Name("username")).SendKeys(login);
    driver.FindElement(By.Name("password")).SendKeys(password);
    driver.FindElement(By.Name("username")).Submit();

    Assert.IsTrue(driver.FindElement(By.TagName("body")).Text.Contains
    (expected_text));

    try
    {
        // if logged in OK, try log out, so next one can continue
        driver.FindElement(By.LinkText("Sign off")).Click();
    }
    catch (Exception ex)
    {
        // ignore
    }
}
```

Identify element IDs with dynamically generated long prefixes

You can use regular expressions to identify the static part of an element ID or name. The following is an HTML fragment for a text box. We could tell some part of ID or name are machine generated (which might be different for the next build), and the part AppName is meaningful.

```
<input id="ctl00_m_g_dcb0d043_e7f0_4128_99c6_71c113f45dd8_ctl00_tAppName_I"
  name="ctl00$m$g_dcb0d043_e7f0_4128_99c6_71c113f45dd8$ctl00$tAppName"/>
```

If we can be sure that AppName is static for each text box, the following test script will work.

```
IWebElement elemByName = driver.FindElement(By.Name("ctl00$m$g_dcb0d043_
e7f0_4128_99c6_71c113f45dd8$ctl00$tAppName"));
elemByName.SendKeys("full name");
elemByName.Clear();
System.Threading.Thread.Sleep(1000);
driver.FindElement(By.XPath("//input[contains(@name, 'AppName')]")).SendKeys
("I still can");
```

Basically it instructs Selenium to find an element whose name attribute contains tAppName.

Sending special keys such as Enter to an element or browser

You can use `driver.SendKeys()` method to send special keys and key combinations to a web control.

```
IWebElement elem = driver.FindElement(By.Id("user"));
elem.Clear();
elem.SendKeys("agileway");
System.Threading.Thread.Sleep(1000); // sleep for seeing the effect

// select all (Ctrl+A) then press backspace
elem.SendKeys(Keys.Control + "A");
elem.SendKeys(Keys.Backspace);
System.Threading.Thread.Sleep(1000);
elem.SendKeys("testwisely");
System.Threading.Thread.Sleep(1000);
elem.SendKeys(Keys.Enter);   //submit the form
```

Use of Unicode in test scripts

Selenium does support Unicode.

```
Assert.AreEqual("空気", driver.FindElement(By.Id("unicode_test")).Text);
driver.FindElement(By.Id("user")).SendKeys("проворный");
```

Extract a group of dynamic data: Verify search results in order

Figure 20-4 shows a sortable table; that is, users can sort table columns in ascending or descending order by clicking the header.

Product ▲	Released	URL
BuildWise	2010	https://testwisely.com/buildwise
ClinicWise	2013	https://clinicwise.net
SiteWise CMS	2014	http://sitewisecms.com
TestWise	2007	https://testwisely.com/testwise

Figure 20-4. *A sortable table*

To verify sorting, we need to extract all the data in the sorted column and then verify the data in the desired order. Knowledge of coding with List or Array is required.

```
driver.FindElement(By.Id("heading_product")).Click(); // sort asc
ReadOnlyCollection<IWebElement> firstCells = driver.FindElements(By.XPath
("//tbody/tr/td[1]"));
List<String> productNames = new List<String>();
foreach (IWebElement elem in firstCells) {; productNames.Add(elem.Text); }
List<String> sortedProductNames = new List<String>(productNames);
sortedProductNames.Sort();
Console.WriteLine(productNames);
Console.WriteLine(sortedProductNames);
Assert.AreEqual(productNames.ToString(), sortedProductNames.ToString());

driver.FindElement(By.Id("heading_product")).Click(); // sort desc
System.Threading.Thread.Sleep(500);
firstCells = driver.FindElements(By.XPath("//tbody/tr/td[1]"));
productNames = new List<String>();
foreach (IWebElement elem in firstCells) { ; productNames.Add(elem.Text); }
sortedProductNames = new List<String>(productNames);
sortedProductNames.Sort();
sortedProductNames.Reverse();
Assert.AreEqual(productNames.ToString(), sortedProductNames.ToString());
```

This approach is not limited to data in tables. The following script extracts the scores from the elements like <span class='score'>98</span>.

```
ReadOnlyCollection scoreElems =
driver.FindElements(By.XPath("//div[@id='results']//span[@class='score']"));
List<String> scores = new List<String>();
foreach (IWebElement elem in scoreElems) { ; scores.Add(elem.Text); }
// ...
```

Verify uniqueness of a set of data

As in the earlier recipe, extract data and store them in an array first, then compare the number of elements in the array with another one without duplicates.

```
ReadOnlyCollection<IWebElement> secondCells;
secondCells = driver.FindElements(By.XPath("//tbody/tr/td[2]"));
List<String> yearsReleased = new List<String>();
foreach (IWebElement elem in secondCells) {; yearsReleased.Add(elem.Text); }
Assert.AreEqual(yearsReleased.Count,new HashSet<String>(yearsReleased).Count);
```

Extract dynamic visible data rows from a results table

Many web search forms have filtering options that hide unwanted result entries (see Figure 20-5).

Product	Released	URL	
ClinicWise	2013	https://clinicwise.net	Like
BuildWise	2010	https://testwisely.com/buildwise	Like
SiteWise CMS	2014	http://sitewisecms.com	Like
TestWise	2007	https://testwisely.com/testwise	Like

Displaying 1 - 4 of 4

Figure 20-5. *Using filtering options*

The following test scripts verify the first product name and click the corresponding "Like" button.

```
driver.Navigate().GoToUrl(TestHelper.SiteUrl() + "/data_grid.html");
ReadOnlyCollection<IWebElement> rows = driver.FindElements(By.XPath
("//table[@id='grid']/tbody/tr"));
Assert.AreEqual(4, rows.Count);
String firstProductName = driver.FindElement(By.XPath("//table[@id='grid']
//tbody/tr[1]/td[1]")).Text;
Assert.AreEqual("ClinicWise", firstProductName);
driver.FindElement(By.XPath("//table[@id='grid']//tbody/tr[1]/td/button")).
Click();
```

Now select the Test Automation Products Only check box, and only two products are shown, as displayed in Figure 20-6.

☑ Test automation products only

Product	Released	URL	
BuildWise	2010	https://testwisely.com/buildwise	Like
TestWise	2007	https://testwisely.com/testwise	Like
		Displaying 1 - 4 of 4	

Figure 20-6. *The result of applying filtering*

```
driver.FindElement(By.Id("test_products_only_flag")).Click();
System.Threading.Thread.Sleep(100);
// Element is not currently visible
driver.FindElement(By.XPath("//table[@id='grid']//tbody/tr[1]/td/button")).
Click();
```

The last test statement would fail with an error Element Is Not Currently Visible. After selecting the Test Automation Products Only check box, we see only two rows on the screen. However, there are still four rows on the page; the other two are hidden (see Figure 20-7).

```
▼ <tbody>
  ▶ <tr class="service_products" style="display: none;"></tr>
  ▶ <tr></tr>
  ▶ <tr class="service_products" style="display: none;"></tr>
  ▶ <tr></tr>
  </tbody>
```

Figure 20-7. *Two filtered rows remain hidden*

The button identified by this XPath //table[@id='grid']//tbody/tr[1]/td/button is now a hidden one, and therefore unable to be clicked.

One solution is to extract the visible rows to an array, and then we could check them by index.

```
ReadOnlyCollection<IWebElement> displayedRows = driver.FindElements
(By.XPath("//table[@id='grid']//tbody/tr[not(contains(@style,'display:
none'))]"));
Assert.AreEqual(2, displayedRows.Count);
IWebElement firstRowElem = displayedRows[0];
```

```
String newFirstProductName = firstRowElem.FindElement(By.XPath("td[1]")).
Text;
Assert.AreEqual("BuildWise", newFirstProductName);
firstRowElem.FindElement(By.XPath("td/button")).Click();
```

Extract dynamic text following a pattern using Regex

To use dynamic data created from the application (e.g., receipt number), we need to extract them. Ideally, those data are marked by dedicated IDs such as <span id='receipt_number'></span>. However, it is not always the case; sometimes the data are mixed in with other text.

The most commonly used approach (in programming) is to extract data with regular expression (Regex). Regex (or regexp) is a pattern of characters that finds matching text. Almost every programming language supports regular expression, with minor differences.

The test script that follows extracts V7H67U and 2015-11-9 from the text Your coupon code: V7H67U used by 2015-11-9, and enter the extracted coupon code in the text box, as shown in Figure 20-8.

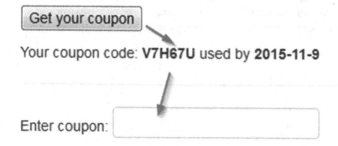

Figure 20-8. *Extracting data with Regex*

```
driver.Navigate().GoToUrl(TestHelper.SiteUrl() + "/coupon.html");
driver.FindElement(By.Id("get_coupon_btn")).Click();
var couponText = driver.FindElement(By.Id("details")).Text;
System.Console.WriteLine(couponText);
Match match = Regex.Match(couponText, @"coupon code:\s+(\w+) used
by\s([\d|-]+)");
if (match.Success)
{
  string coupon = match.Groups[1].Value;
  string expiryDate = match.Groups[2].Value;
```

```
  // System.Console.WriteLine(coupon);
  driver.FindElement(By.Name("coupon")).SendKeys(coupon);
}
else {
  throw new Exception("Error: no valid coupon returned");
}
```

Regex is very powerful and it does take some time to master it. To get it going for simple text matching, however, is not hard. Searching "C# regular expression" will find your good tutorials. RegexPlanet (`http://www.regexplanet.com/advanced/dotnet/`) is a helpful tool to let you try Regex online.

CHAPTER 21

■ ■ ■

Optimization

Working test scripts are just the first test step to successful test automation, as automated tests are executed often, and we all know the application changes frequently, too. Therefore, it is important that our test scripts be

- Fast

- Easy to read

- Concise

In this chapter, I show some examples to optimize test scripts.

Assert string in page_source is faster than the text

To verify a piece of text on a web page, frequently for assertion, we can use `driver.PageSource` or `driver.FindElement(By.TagName("body")).Text`. Besides the obvious different output, there are major performance differences, too. To get a text view (for a whole page or a web control), WebDriver needs to analyze the raw HTML to generate the text view, and it takes time. We usually do not notice that time when the raw HTML is small. However, for a large web page like the WebDriver standard (over 430 KB in file size), incorrect use of text view will slow your test execution significantly.

```
driver.Navigate().GoToUrl(TestHelper.SiteUrl() + "/WebDriverStandard.html");
var watch = Stopwatch.StartNew();
String checkText = "language-neutral wire protocol";
Assert.IsTrue(driver.FindElement(By.TagName("body")).Text.
Contains(checkText));
watch.Stop();
var elapsedSec = watch.ElapsedMilliseconds / 1000.0;
Console.WriteLine("Method 1: Search page text took " + elapsedSec + " seconds");

watch = Stopwatch.StartNew();
Assert.IsTrue(driver.PageSource.Contains(checkText));
elapsedSec = watch.ElapsedMilliseconds / 1000.0;
Console.WriteLine("Method 2: Search page HTML took " + elapsedSec + " seconds");
```

135

Output

```
Method 1: Search page text took 8.44 seconds
Method 2: Search page HTML took 0.17 seconds
```

Getting text from more specific elements is faster

A rule of thumb is that we save execution time by narrowing down a more specific control. The two assertion statements below largely achieve the same purpose but with a significant difference in execution time.

```
String checkText = "language-neutral wire protocol";
Assert.IsTrue(driver.FindElement(By.TagName("body")).Text.Contains(checkText));
```

Execution time: **8.44** seconds

```
Assert.IsTrue(driver.FindElement(By.Id("abstract")).Text.Contains(checkText));
```

Execution time: **0.05** seconds

Avoid programming if-else block code if possible

Programmers commonly write test scripts in a similar way as coding applications. Although I cannot say it is wrong, I prefer simple, concise, and easy-to-read test scripts. Whenever possible, I prefer one line of test statement matching one user operation. This can be quite helpful when debugging test scripts. For example, by using ternary operator ? :, these six lines of test statements

```
if (refNo.Contains("VIP")) { // Special
  Assert.AreEqual("Go upstair", driver.FindElement(By.Id("notes")).Text);
}
else
{
  Assert.AreEqual("", driver.FindElement(By.Id("notes")).Text);
}
```

can be reduced to one.

```
Assert.AreEqual(refNo.Contains("VIP") ? "Go upstair" : "", driver.
FindElement(By.Id("notes")).Text);
```

Use variable to cache unchanged data

Commonly, I saw people writing tests like this one to check multiple texts on a page.

```
driver.Navigate().GoToUrl(TestHelper.SiteUrl() + "/WebDriverStandard.html");
Assert.IsTrue(driver.FindElement(By.TagName("body")).Text.
Contains("Firefox"));
Assert.IsTrue(driver.FindElement(By.TagName("body")).Text.
Contains("chrome"));
Assert.IsTrue(driver.FindElement(By.TagName("body")).Text.Contains("W3C"));
```

Execution time: **25.9** seconds

These three test statements are very inefficient, as every test statement calls `driver.FindElement(By.TagName("body")).Text`. This can be quite an expensive operation when a web page is large.

The solution is to use a variable to store the text (view) of the web page, a very common practice in programming.

```
var thePageText = driver.FindElement(By.TagName("body")).Text;
Assert.IsTrue(thePageText.Contains("Firefox"));
Assert.IsTrue(thePageText.Contains("chrome"));
Assert.IsTrue(thePageText.Contains("W3C"));
```

Execution time: **8.3** seconds

As you can see, we get quite constant execution time no matter how many assertions we perform on that page, as long as the page text we are checking is not changing.

Enter large text into a text box

We commonly use `SendKeys` to enter text into a text box. When the text string you want to enter is quite large, for example, thousands of characters, try to avoid using `SendKeys`, as it is not efficient. Here is an example.

```
string longText= new string('*', 5000);
IWebElement textArea = driver.FindElement(By.Id("comments"));
textArea.SendKeys(longText);
```

Execution time: **3.8** seconds.

When this test is executed in Chrome, you can see a batch of text "typed" into the text box. Furthermore, there might be a limited number of characters that WebDriver can "send" into a text box for browsers at one time. I have seen test scripts that broke long text into trunks and then sent them one by one, which is not elegant.

The solution is actually quite simple using JavaScript.

```
((IJavaScriptExecutor)driver).ExecuteScript("document.
getElementById('comments').value = arguments[0];", longText);
```

. Execution time: **0.02** seconds

Use environment variables to change test behaviors dynamically

Typically, there is more than one test environment we need to run automated tests against, and we might want to run the same test in different browsers now and then. I saw test scripts like this one often in projects.

```
static IWebDriver driver;
//..
static String siteRootUrl = "http://physio.clinicwise.net";
// static String siteRootUrl = "http://yake.clinicwise.net";

driver = new ChromeDriver();
// driver = new FirefoxDriver();
driver.Navigate().GoToUrl(siteRootUrl);
```

It works like this: Testers comment and uncomment a set of test statements to let the test script run against different servers in different browsers. This is not an ideal approach, because it is inefficient and error prone, and it introduces unnecessary check-ins (changing test script files with no changes to testing logic).

A simple solution is to use agreed environment variables, so that the target server URL and browser type can be set externally, outside the test scripts.

```
String browserTypeSetInEnv = Environment.GetEnvironmentVariable("BROWSER");
Console.WriteLine(browserTypeSetInEnv);
if (!String.IsNullOrEmpty(browserTypeSetInEnv) &&
browserTypeSetInEnv.Equals("chrome"))
{
    driver = new ChromeDriver();
} else
{
    driver = new FirefoxDriver();
}

if (!String.IsNullOrWhiteSpace(Environment.GetEnvironmentVariable("SITE_URL")))
{
    siteRootUrl = Environment.GetEnvironmentVariable("SITE_URL");
}
driver.Navigate().GoToUrl(siteRootUrl);
```

For example, to run this test against another server in Chrome, run the following commands.

```
> set BROWSER=chrome
> set SITE_URL=http://yake.clinicwise.net
```

Followed by the test execution command, the test will run against new site URL on Chrome. This approach is commonly used in the continuous testing process. Please note that the environment variable values are cached in a process. For example, if you modified the environment variables in System Properties, you need to restart Visual Studio for those changes to take effect.

Test a web app in two languages

The following test scripts test user authentication for two test sites, the same application in two languages: http://physio.clinicwise.net in English and http://yake.clinicwise.net in Chinese. Although the business features are the same, the text shown on two sites are different, and so are the test user accounts.

```
driver.Navigate().GoToUrl(siteRootUrl); // may be dynamically set

if (siteRootUrl.Contains("physio.clinicwise.net"))
{
  driver.FindElement(By.Id("username")).SendKeys("natalie");
  driver.FindElement(By.Id("password")).SendKeys("test");
  driver.FindElement(By.Id("signin_button")).Click();
  Assert.IsTrue(driver.PageSource.Contains("Signed in successfully."));
}
else if (siteRootUrl.Contains("yake.clinicwise.net"))
{
  driver.FindElement(By.Id("username")).SendKeys("tuo");
  driver.FindElement(By.Id("password")).SendKeys("test");
  driver.FindElement(By.Id("signin_button")).Click();
  Assert.IsTrue(driver.PageSource.Contains("成功登录"));
}
```

Although the preceding test scripts work, the process seems lengthy and repetitive.

```
public bool IsChinese()
{
    return siteRootUrl.Contains("yake.clinicwise.net");
}

[TestMethod]
public void TestTwoLanguagesUsingTernaryOperator()
{
  driver = new ChromeDriver();
  driver.Navigate().GoToUrl(siteRootUrl); // may be dynamically set

  driver.FindElement(By.Id("username")).SendKeys(IsChinese() ? "tuo" : "natalie");
  driver.FindElement(By.Id("password")).SendKeys("test");
```

```
driver.FindElement(By.Id("signin_button")).Click();
Assert.IsTrue(driver.PageSource.Contains( IsChinese() ? "成功登录" :
"Signed in successfully."));
}
```

HINT: USING IDS CAN GREATLY SAVE MULTILANGUAGE TESTING

When doing multilanguage testing, try not to use the actual text on the page for non-user-entered operations. For example, the test statements are not optimal.

```
driver.FindElement(By.LinkText("Register")).Click();
// or below with some programming logic ...
driver.FindElement(By.LinkText("Registre")).Click();  // French
driver.FindElement(By.LinkText("注册")).Click();  // Chinese
```

Using IDs is much simpler.

```
driver.FindElement(By.Id("register_link")).Click();
```

This works for all languages.

Multi-language testing with lookups

This following test script is to test the same application against three different deployed servers in different languages, with the same version of test script.

```
// return the current language used on the site
public string SiteLang()
{
    if (siteRootUrl.Contains("yake.clinicwise.net"))
    {
        return "chinese";
    } else if (siteRootUrl.Contains("sandbox.clinicwise.net"))
    {
        return "french";
    } else
    {
        return "english";
    }
}
```

```
// in test case
if (SiteLang() == "chinese")
{
    driver.FindElement(By.Id("username")).SendKeys("tuo");
}
else if (SiteLang() == "french")
{
    driver.FindElement(By.Id("username")).SendKeys("dupont");
}
else { // default
    driver.FindElement(By.Id("username")).SendKeys("natalie");
}
driver.FindElement(By.Id("password")).SendKeys("test");
driver.FindElement(By.Id("signin_button")).Click();
```

If this is going to be used only once, this is fine. However, these login test steps will be used heavily, which will lead to lengthy and hard-to-maintain test scripts.

The solution is to centralize the logic with lookups.

```
public String UserLookup(string username)
{
  switch (SiteLang())
  {
    case "chinese":
      return "tuo";

    case "french":
      return "dupont";
    default:
      return username;
  }
}
```

```
// in test case
driver.FindElement(By.Id("username")).SendKeys(UserLookup("natalie"));
```

Astute readers might point out that I have oversimplified the cases, and there surely will be more test users. Yes, that's true. I was trying to use the simplest way to convey the lookup concept. Here is a more complete solution.

```
private static readonly Dictionary<string, string> natalieUserDict = new
Dictionary<string, string> {
    { "english", "natalie" },
    { "chinese", "tuo" },
    { "french", "dupont" }
};
```

```
private static readonly Dictionary<string, string> markUserDict = new
Dictionary<string, string> {
    { "english", "mark" },
    { "chinese", "li" },
    { "french", "marc" }
};

public String UserLookupDict(string username)
{
  switch (username)
  {
    case "natalie":
      return natalieUserDict[SiteLang()];

    case "mark":
      return markUserDict[SiteLang()];

    default:
      return username;
  }
}

// In test case
driver.FindElement(By.Id("username")).SendKeys(UserLookupDict("natalie"));
```

In summary, the test user in a chosen language (English in this example) is used as the key to look up for other languages. The equivalent user of "natalie" in French is "dupont".

Some, typically programmers, write test scripts like this.

```
public String GetAdminUser() {
  // logic goes here
}

driver.FindElement(By.Id("username")).SendKeys(GetAdminUser());
```

If there are only a handful users, it might be okay. Often, though, I see hard-to-read test statements such as GetRegisteredUser1() and GetManager2(). Who is Manager2? Some test scripts go further to read test users from external configuration files, which are hard to maintain.

CHAPTER 22

Gotchas

For the most part, the Selenium WebDriver API is quite straightforward. Here is a one-sentence summary: Find an element and perform an operation on it. Writing test scripts in Selenium WebDriver is much more than knowing the API; it involves programming, HTML, JavaScript, and web browsers. There are cases that can be confusing to newcomers.

Test starts browser but no execution with blank screen

A very possible cause of this problem is that the version of Selenium WebDriver installed is not compatible with the version of your browser. Figure 22-1 is a screenshot of Firefox 41.0.2 started by a Selenium WebDriver 2.44.0 test.

Figure 22-1. *Firefox started by a Selenium WebDriver test*

The test hung there. After I upgraded Selenium WebDriver to 2.45, the test ran fine.

This can happen to Chrome, too. With both browsers and Selenium WebDriver being updated quite frequently, in a matter of months, it is not that surprising to encounter incompatibility issues. For test engineers who are not aware of this, it can be quite confusing, as the tests might be running fine the day before and no changes have been made since.

Once you know the cause, the solutions are easy.

- Upgrade both Selenium WebDriver and browsers to the latest version. Browsers such as Chrome usually turn on automatic upgrades by default. I suggest upgrading to the latest Selenium WebDriver several days after it is released.

- Lock Selenium WebDriver and browsers. Turn off automatic upgrades in the browser and be thoughtful on upgrading Selenium WebDriver.

Be aware of browser and driver changes

One day I found over 40 test failures (out of about 400) by surprise on the latest continuous testing build. There were few changes since the last build, in which all tests passed. I quickly figured out the cause: Chrome autoupgraded to version 44. Chrome 44 with the ChromeDriver 2.17 changed the behavior of clicking hyperlinks. After clicking a link, sometimes test executions immediately continue to the next operation without waiting for the "clicking link" operation to finish.

```
driver.FindElement(By.Id("new_client")).Click();
// workaround for chrome v44, make sure the link is clicked
System.Threading.Thread.Sleep(1000);
```

A week later, I noticed the only line in the change log of ChromeDriver v2.18:

```
"Changes include many bug fixes that allow ChromeDriver to work more
reliably with Chrome 44+."
```

Failed to assert copied text in browser

To answer this, let's start with an example. What we see in a browser like Internet Explorer (Figure 22-2) is the result of rendering the page source (HTML) shown in Figure 22-3 in Internet Explorer.

BOLD *Italic*

```
Text assertion
(new line before)!
```

Figure 22-2. How text appears in a browser

```
<p id="text"> <b>BOLD</b>  <i>Italic</i></p>
```

```
<pre id="formatted">Text assertion  
(new line before)!</pre>
```

Figure 22-3. *The HTML that creates the text in the browser*

As you can see, there are differences. Test scripts can be written to check the text view (what we saw) on browsers or its raw page source (HTML). To complicate things a little more, old versions of browsers might return slightly different results.

Do not worry, as long as you understand that the text shown in browsers is coming from raw HTML source code. After a few attempts, this is usually not a problem. Here are the test scripts for checking text and source for the preceding example.

```
driver.Url = "http://testwisely.com/demo/assertion";
// tags in source not in text
Assert.IsTrue(driver.FindElement(By.TagName("body")).Text.Contains("BOLD
Italic"));
Assert.IsTrue(driver.PageSource.Contains("<b>BOLD</b>  <i>Italic</i>"));
// HTML entities in source but shown as space in text
Assert.IsTrue(driver.FindElement(By.TagName("body")).Text.
Contains("assertion  \r\n(new line before)"));
// note the second character after assertion is nonbreakable space ( )

Assert.IsTrue(driver.PageSource.Contains("assertion  \r\n(new line
before)"));
```

The same test works for Chrome, but not for Internet Explorer

Chrome, Firefox, and Internet Explorer are different products and web browsers are very complex software. Comparing to other testing frameworks, Selenium WebDriver provides best support for all major browsers. Still there will be some operations that work differently on one than another.

```
ICapabilities caps = ((RemoteWebDriver)driver).Capabilities;
String browserName = caps.BrowserName;
if (browserName == "chrome")
{
  // chrome specific test statement
}
else if (browserName == "firefox")
{
  // firefox specific test statement
}
```

145

```
else
{
  throw new Exception("Unsupported browser: " + browserName);
}
```

Some might say that it will require a lot of work. Yes, cross-browser testing is associated with more testing effort, obviously. However, from my observation, few IT managers acknowledge this. That's why cross-testing is talked about a lot, but rarely gets done.

"Unexpected tag name 'input'"

This is because there is another control matching your FindElement and it is a different control type (input tag). For example:

```
<input type="checkbox" name="vip" value="on"> VIP?

<!-- ... -->
<select name="vip"/>
  <option value="true">Yes</option>
  <option value="false">No/option>
</select>
```

The intention of the following test script is to select 'Yes' in the drop-down list, unaware of another check box control sharing exactly the same name attribute.

```
IWebElement elem = driver.FindElement(By.Name("vip"));
SelectElement select = new SelectElement(elem);
select.SelectByValue("Yes");
```

Here is the error returned:

```
'ArgumentError: unexpected tag name "input"'
```

The solution is quite obvious after you know the cause: change the locators; that is, driver.FindElement(By.XPath("//select[@name='vip']"));.

Here is another similar (and more common) scenario: A hidden element and a check box element share the same ID and NAME attributes.

```
<input type="hidden" name="vip" value="false"/>
<!-- ... -->
<input type="checkbox" name="vip" value="on"> VIP?
```

In this case, there might be no error thrown. However, this can be more subtle, as the operation is applied to a different control.

Element is not clickable or not visible

For some controls -+such as text fields, even when they are not visible in the current browser window, Selenium WebDriver will move the focus to them. For some other controls, such as buttons, this might not be the case. In that situation, although the element is found by FindElement, it is not clickable.

The solution is to make the target control visible in the browser.

1. Scroll the window to make the control visible. Find out the control's position and scroll to it.

```
IWebElement elem = driver.FindElement(By.Name("submit_action_2"));
int elemPos = elem.Location.Y;
((IJavaScriptExecutor)driver).ExecuteScript("window.scroll(0, " + elemPos + ");");
```

Or scroll to the top or bottom of the page.

```
String js = "window.scrollTo(0, document.body.scrollHeight);";
((IJavaScriptExecutor)driver).ExecuteScript(js);
```

2. A hack, call send_keys to a text field nearby, if there is one.

```
driver.FindElement(By.Name("top_checkbox")).Click();
// the focus in the on the top
IWebElement nextBtn = driver.FindElement(By.Id("next_btn"));
// found but not visible, unable to click
// find a nearby text field
driver.FindElement(By.Name("age")).SendKeys("");
nextBtn.Click();
```

■ ■ ■

CHAPTER 23

Remote Control Server

Selenium Server, formerly known as Selenium Remote Control Server, allows testers to write Selenium tests in their favorite language and execute them on another machine. The word *remote* means that the test scripts and the target browser might not be on the same machine.

Selenium Server is composed of two parts: a server and a client.

- *Selenium Server*: A Java server that launches, drives, and kills browsers on receiving commands, with the target browser installed on the machine.

- *Client libraries*: Test scripts in a Selenium's language binding, such as C#, Java, Ruby, and Python.

Selenium Server installation

Make sure you have Java Runtime installed first. Download Selenium Server (selenium-server-standalone-{VERSION}.jar) from the Selenium download page and place it on the computer with the browser(s) you want to test. From the directory with the .jar file, run the following command from Command Prompt:

```
java -jar selenium-server-standalone-2.44.0.jar
```

Sample output

```
08:59:07.856 INFO - Launching a standalone server
08:59:07.919 INFO - Java: Apple Inc. 20.65-b04-466.1
08:59:07.919 INFO - OS: Mac OS X 10.10.1 x86_64
08:59:07.935 INFO - v2.44.0, with Core v2.44.0. Built from revision 76d78cf
```

There are two options you can pass to the server: timeout and browserTimeout.

```
java -jar selenium-server-standalone-2.44.0.jar -timeout=20 -browserTimeout=60
```

Execute tests in the specified browser on another machine

There are a few prerequisites to executing the tests.

- Make sure Selenium Server is up and running.

- You can connect to the server via HTTP.

- Note the server machine's IP address.

Changing existing local Selenium tests (running on a local browser) to remote Selenium tests (running on a remote browser) is very easy. Just update the initialization of the WebDriver instance to RemoteWebDriver as shown here.

```
static IWebDriver driver;

[TestInitialize]
public static void BeforeAll()
{
    try
    {
        DesiredCapabilities capabilities = DesiredCapabilities.Firefox();
        driver = new RemoteWebDriver(capabilities);
    }
    catch (Exception ex)
    {
        Console.WriteLine("ex = " + ex);
    }
}

[TestInitialize]
public void Before()
{
    driver.Navigate().GoToUrl("http://testwisely.com/demo/netbank");
}

[TestMethod]
public void TestExplicitWaitsInRemoteBrowser()
{
    SelectElement select = new SelectElement(driver.FindElement(By.
    Name("account")));
    select.SelectByText("Cheque");
    driver.FindElement(By.Id("rcptAmount")).SendKeys("250");
    driver.FindElement(By.XPath("//input[@value='Transfer']")).Click();
```

```
    WebDriverWait wait = new WebDriverWait(driver, TimeSpan.
FromSeconds(10));  // seconds
    wait.Until(d => d.FindElement(By.Id("receiptNo")));
}

[TestMethod]
public void TestImplicitWaitsInRemoteBrowser()
{
    SelectElement select = new SelectElement(driver.FindElement(By.
Name("account")));
    select.SelectByText("Cheque");
    driver.FindElement(By.Id("rcptAmount")).SendKeys("250");
    driver.FindElement(By.XPath("//input[@value='Transfer']")).Click();
    driver.Manage().Timeouts().ImplicitlyWait(TimeSpan.FromSeconds(10));
    Assert.IsTrue(driver.FindElement(By.Id("receiptNo")).Text.Length > 0);
    // reset for later steps
    driver.Manage().Timeouts().ImplicitlyWait(TimeSpan.FromSeconds(1));
}

[TestCleanup]
public void After()
{
}

[ClassCleanup]
public static void AfterAll()
{
    driver.Quit();
}
```

The test script (client) is expected to terminate each browser session properly, calling driver.Quit().

Selenium Grid

Selenium Grid allows you to run Selenium tests in parallel to cut down the execution time. Selenium Grid includes one hub and many nodes.

Start the hub

The hub receives the test requests and distributes them to the nodes.

```
java -jar selenium-server-standalone-2.44.0.jar -role hub
```

Start the nodes

A node gets tests from the hub and runs them.

```
java -jar selenium-server-standalone-2.44.0.jar -role node -hub
http://localhost:4444/grid/register
```

If you start a node on another machine, replace localhost with the hub's IP address.

Using Grid to run tests

You need to change the test script to point to the driver to the hub.

```
DesiredCapabilities capabilities = DesiredCapabilities.Chrome();
driver = new RemoteWebDriver(new Uri("http://127.0.0.1:4444/wd/hub"),
capabilities);
// ...
```

The test will run on one of the nodes. Please note that the timing and test case counts (from RSpec) returned are apparently not right.

Frankly, I haven't yet met anyone who is able to show me a working Selenium Grid running a fair number of UI Selenium tests.

Concerns with Selenium Grid

- Complexity

  For every Selenium Grid node, you need to configure the node either by specifying command-line parameters or a JSON file. Check out the Grid Wiki page for details.

  It is my understanding that after just pushing the tests to the hub, it handles the rest based on the configuration. My experience tells me that is too good to be true. For example, here is an error I got.

  ```
  [remote server] com.google.common.base.
  Preconditions(Preconditions.java):177:in `checkState':
  The path to the driver executable must be set by the
  webdriver.chrome.driver system property; for more
  information, see http://code.google.com/p/selenium/
  wiki/ChromeDriver. The latest version can be downloaded
  from http://chromedriver.storage.googleapis.com/index.
  html (java.lang.IllegalStateException) (Selenium::WebDr
  iver::Error::UnknownError)
  ```

  The error message is quite clear: No ChromeDriver is installed. But on which node? Shouldn't the hub know about that?

- Very limited control

  Selenium Grid comes with a very basic web-accessible console. For instance, I created two nodes: one on a Macintosh and the other on a system running Windows 7 (the console displayed as VISTA). The results are shown in Figure 23-1.

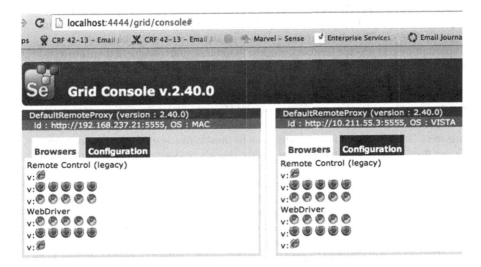

Figure 23-1. *The Selenium Grid console*

  An Internet Explorer icon for for Mac node? This does not seem right.

- Lack of feedback

  UI tests take time to execute, and more tests means longer execution time. Selenium Grid's distribution model is to reduce that. Apart from the raw execution time, there is also the feedback time. The team would like to see the test results as soon as a test execution finishes on one node. Even better, when we pass the whole test suite to the hub, it will intelligently run new or last failed tests first. Selenium Grid, in my view, falls short on this.

- Lack of rerun

  In a perfect world, all tests execute as expected every single time. In reality, though, there are many factors that could affect the test execution. Here are just a few:

  - Test statements didn't wait long enough for AJAX requests to complete (server on load).

  - Browser crashes (it happens).

- Node runs out of disk space.

- Virus scanning process started in background.

- Windows auto updates.

In this case, reassigning failed tests to anther node could save a potentially good build.

My point is this: I could quickly put together a demo with Selenium Grid running tests on different nodes (with different browsers), and the audience might be quite impressed. However, in reality, when you have a large number of UI test suites, the game is totally different. The whole process needs to be simple, stable, flexible, and most important, able to provide feedback quickly. In the true spirit of Agile, if there are tests failing, no code shall be allowed to check in. Now we are talking about the pressure.

How to achieve distributed test execution over multiple browsers? First of all, distributed test execution and cross-browser testing are two different things. Distributed test execution speeds up test execution (it could be just against single type of browser), whereas cross-browser testing is to verify the application's ability to work on a range of browsers. Yes, distributed test execution can be used to test against different browsers. Do get distributed test execution done solidly, though, before worrying about the cross-browser testing.

I firmly believe the UI test execution with feedback should be a part of a CI process, just like running xUnit tests and the report shown on the CI server. It is okay for developers and testers to develop Selenium tests in an IDE, in which they run one or a handful tests often. However, executing a large number of UI tests, which is time consuming, should be done on the CI server.

The purpose of a perfect CI process is building the application to pass all tests, to be ready for production release. Distributed execution of UI tests with quick feedback, in my opinion, is an important feature of a CI server. However, most CI servers on the market do not support this feature. You can find more information on this topic in my other book, *Practical Web Test Automation*.

CHAPTER 24

Afterword

First of all, if you haven't downloaded the recipe test scripts from the book site, I strongly recommend that you do so.

Practice makes perfect

Like any other skills, you will get better by practicing more.

Write tests

Many testers would like to practice test automation with Selenium WebDriver, but they don't have a good target application to write tests against. Here I have made one of my applications available for you: ClinicWise Sandbox (http:///sandbox.clinicwise.net). ClinicWise is a modern web application using popular web technologies such as AJAX and Bootstrap. I have written and been maintaining 445 Selenium WebDriver tests for ClinicWise. Execution of all tests takes more than four hours on a single machine. If you like, you can certainly practice writing tests against the ClinicWise sandbox.

ClinicWise is also a showcase of web applications designed for testing, which means it is easier to write automated tests against it. Every Selenium test starts with calling a database reset: Visit http:///sandbox.clinicwise.net/reset, which will reset the database to a seeded state (see Figure 24-1).

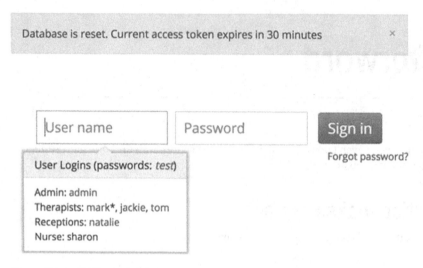

Figure 24-1. *Calling a database reset*

Improve programming skills

Programming skills are required to use Selenium WebDriver effectively. For readers with no programming background, the good news is that the programming knowledge required for writing test scripts is much less compared to coding applications, as you have seen in this book.

Successful test automation

I believe that you are well equipped to cope with most testing scenarios if you have mastered the recipes in this book. However, this only applies to your ability to write individual tests. Successful test automation also requires developing and maintaining many automated test cases even as software applications change frequently.

Maintain test scripts to keep up with application changes

Let's say you have 100 automated tests that all pass. The changes developers made in the next build will affect some of your tests. As this happens too often, many automated tests will fail. The only way to keep the test script maintainable is to adopt good test design practices (e.g., reusable functions and page objects) and efficient refactoring. Check out my other book, *Practical Web Test Automation.*

Shorten test execution time to get quick feedback

With a growing number of test cases, test execution time also increases. This leads to a long feedback gap from the time programmers commit the code to the time test execution completes. If programmers continue to develop new features and fixes during the gap time, it can easily develop into a tail-chasing problem. This will hurt the team's productivity badly. Executing automated tests in a continuous testing server with various techniques (e.g., distributing tests to run in parallel) can greatly shorten the feedback time. *Practical Web Test Automation* includes one chapter on this.

Best wishes for your test automation!

■ ■ ■

CHAPTER 25

Resources

Books

- *Practical Web Test Automation* by Zhimin Zhan

- Solving individual Selenium challenges (what this book is for) is far from achieving test automation success. *Practical Web Test Automation* is the book to guide you to test automation success. The topics include the following:

  - Developing easy-to-read and maintain Watir/Selenium tests using next-generation functional testing tool.

  - Page object model.

  - Functional testing refactorings.

  - Cross-browser testing against Internet Explorer, Firefox, and Chrome.

  - Setting up continuous testing server to manage execution of a large number of automated UI tests.

  - Requirement traceability matrix.

  - Strategies on team collaboration and test automation adoption in projects and organizations.

Web sites

- **Selenium .NET API** http://selenium.googlecode.com/git/docs/api/dotnet/index.html

- **Selenium Home** http://seleniumhq.org

Tools

- **Visual Studio** http://www.visualstudio.com/en-US/products/visual-studio-express-vs

- **NUnit, a unit testing framework for .NET** http://www.nunit.org/

Index

Get the eBook for only $5!

Why limit yourself?

Now you can take the weightless companion with you wherever you go and access your content on your PC, phone, tablet, or reader.

Since you've purchased this print book, we're happy to offer you the eBook in all 3 formats for just $5.

Convenient and fully searchable, the PDF version enables you to easily find and copy code—or perform examples by quickly toggling between instructions and applications. The MOBI format is ideal for your Kindle, while the ePUB can be utilized on a variety of mobile devices.

To learn more, go to www.apress.com/companion or contact support@apress.com.

Apress®
THE EXPERT'S VOICE™

Printed in the United States
By Bookmasters